Extension: The Third Dimension of Higher Education

About the Author

Dr. Erbanoris Jyrwa is presently Reader and Head, Centre for Adult and Continuing Education, School of Humanities and Education, NEHU, Shillong. She has published one book *Administration of Justice in the Khasi Hills* (2006) and has co-edited two books, viz. *Adult Education Programmes for Development* (2007) and *Female Emancipation: Trends and Issues in North East India* (2008). Also, she has to her credit over 40 Academic papers, Research articles published in various journals of repute. She has presented papers in national and international seminars as well.

Dr. Jyrwa has directed and completed four research projects sponsored by University Grants Commission on Population Education Programmes and Impact of Adult Education Programmes and by National Council of Rural Institute (NCRI), NHRD, New Delhi to conduct a survey to identify the Need-based Short-term Continuing Education Courses and Development of Innovative Continuing Education Courses.

EXTENSION

The Third Dimension of Higher Education

Erbanoris Jyrwa

CONCEPT PUBLISHING COMPANY, NEW DELHI-110 059

Cataloging in Publication Data—DK
Courtesy: D.K. Agencies (P) Ltd. <docinfo@dkagencies.com>

Jyrwa, Erbanoris, 1962-
Extension: the thrid dimension of higher education/Erbanoris Jyrwa.
p. cm.
Study conducted in Meghalaya, India.
Includes bibliographical references.
Includes index.
ISBN 13: 9788180695544
ISBN 10: 8180695549

1. Adult education—India—Meghalaya. 2. Rural extension—India—Meghalaya. 3. University extension—Social aspects—India Meghalaya. 4. Population—Study and teaching—India—Meghalaya. 5. Education and state—India—Meghalaya. I. Title.

DDC 374.954 164 22

ISBN-13: 978-81-8069-554-4
ISBN-10: 81-8069-554-9

First Published 2008

Published and Printed by
Ashok Kumar Mittal
Concept Publishing Company
A/15-16, Commercial Block, Mohan Garden
New Delhi (INDIA)

Phones : 25351460, 25351794
Fax : 091-11-25357103
Email : publishing@conceptpub.com

Preface

Extension is a very broad concept. In the context of Higher Education "**Extension**" means to reach out to a wider clientele through a process of extending knowledge, beyond the four walls of the University. Historically, the term extension was first used in USA with reference to Land Grant Colleges, extending knowledge to farmers. Later, the term extension was expanded to include other subjects and fields like Agricultural extension, Home Science extension, Nutrition extension, Sanitation extension, Industrial extension and so on.

The essence of extension education is to change the attitudes and practices of people with whom the work is done. University extension represents attempts to extend educational opportunities to those who have not been able to attend institutions of Higher learning and also to render specialized educational services to different sections of society. The resources of the University are made available to the community at large and as a result also bring the concerns of the society to the attention of the scholars of the University.

Extension education includes Adult Education, Continuing Education, Population Education, Community Education, etc. The Extension and Field Outreach activities aims to promote a meaningful and sustained rapport between Universities and communities, consisting of all age groups. The entire higher education system in India is in the process of transformation to cater to the needs of the students in particular and community in general. The Socio-Economic, Scientific, and Cultural development of a country depends on the quality of the population. The quality of the population depends upon the type of education system prevailing in our country.

The University Grants Commission in their policy framework of Higher Education recognized Extension and

Field Outreach as the third dimension of the institution of Higher Education by ensuring that the University system will propagate life long learning. The UGC has accepted Teaching, Research, Extension and Field Outreach as the three major functions of Higher Education. The UGC's guidelines 2004 on Adult and Continuing Education underlined the need for Extension activities by the Higher Education system.

The application of knowledge in real life situation is possible through Extension and Field Outreach activities, which will further generate knowledge. Higher Education is envisaged as an instrument of social transformation. In higher education, universities expected to perform a very crucial role in promoting social change. The universities need to facilitate the development of capabilities of the community for the overall development of the nation and help the community to improve quality of life.

The third dimension aims to promote a meaningful and sustained rapport between the Colleges/Universities and the community. The acceptance of extension as the third dimension, equal in importance to teaching and research was in the context of a growing realization that the Universities and Colleges have institutional resources—knowledge, man power and physical—have the obligation to develop sensitivities to involve the development of the community with particular reference to overall and diverse learning needs of all segments of the people of the community.

One of the major thrusts by the UGC in the Tenth Plan period on Adult and Continuing Education is to address the Social issues like Adult literacy, School drop-outs, Child labour, Mal-nutrition, Environmental problems, Gender issues, Family life education, HIV/AIDS, Women Empowerment, Human Rights education, Consumer Rights and Self-employment.

The Centre for Adult and Continuing Education is the connecting link between the university and society, which ensures the campus to Community and University-Industry collaborative programmes through Field Outreach Activities. Knowledge can be generated by the teaching departments and centres alike. But Centres like Adult and Continuing Education take up another responsibility of disseminating knowledge to the Community through Extension and Field Outreach Activities.

Extension and Field Outreach have the potential to become the driving force behind the successful activities of a University. The primary way in which society can be informed of knowledge and break through in Science, Engineering, Technology, Humanities, Languages, Social Sciences, Agriculture and many other such fields of endeavour at Universities is through the Extension activities of the University. In the modern age, when Global communication is nearly instantaneous and society is more urban and suburban, change in Extension and Field Outreach has become essential. One mechanism for increasing involvement and awareness of extension activities would be to encourage more faculties to participate in extension activities.

The major objectives of third dimension are:

- —To extend Knowledge and other institutional resources to the community and *vice versa*.
- —To gain insights from a contact between Knowledge, Resources and Socio-Cultural relations to reflect these in the entire curricular system of Higher Education.
- —To help students to face life and its challenges.

It is to be noted that communities in the rural, urban and slum areas are facing different types of problems. Most of the problems are related to lack of awareness and poor skills among the people. Many of the problems of the society and especially the poor can be solved very easily if we plan in a systematic way.

It is pertinent to state that all the Universities/Colleges and other educational establishments have several aspects, viz. information, skills, technology, service, and so on. But the institutional structures are not oriented to extend the best to the society. Further, the institutions do not have the mechanism to convert the available extendable in a form suitable to the requirements of the community. Every University/Department/ Centre can deeply involve in extension activities, provided they should know the strategy and the method.

This book consists of Fifteen Research papers which deal mainly with the Issues and Perspective in Adult and Field Outreach to transform communities by responding to their needs. The studies on Adult Education pointed out that the programme did not create qualitative impact in the learners especially in the areas of awareness and skills. It is in this context that the present study is initiated and conducted.

The contents of the book provide an indepth view of the extension programmes undertaken by the author in different villages of the state of Meghalaya and on Research projects undertaken with the financial support from University Grants Commission, Delhi. The main study attempts to quantify the impact of Adult education programme in the development of literacy skills, population issues, women issues, environmental issues and issues relating to social awareness among the clientele representing various implementing agencies such as Universities, Voluntary Organizations and Government wings. The book highlights the experience, successful achievements and difficulties in the implementation of Extension—The Third Dimension of Higher Education. The author received considerable support and co-operation from several traditional heads of the villages, individuals and concerned people who know the work.

I am thankful to Prof. B. Vijayakumar, Member UGC Expert Committee on Adult Continuing Education, Extension and Field Outreach for his valuable information in completing this endeavour. The untiring support extended by my dear parents, brothers and sisters, who took up and shared in all the family responsibilities, thereby enable me to concentrate on my research work totally. Finally, my sincere thanks go to the Concept Publishing Company, New Delhi for their acceptance in publishing the book.

I fervently hope that this handy volume will be very much useful to extension professionals, academicians, curriculum designers, adult education functionaries, student communities and the general public at large to know about the research findings, innovations, experiences and exchange views in the above field.

Erbanoris Jyrwa

Contents

SECTION IV

EXTENSION EDUCATION: IMPACT ON LITERACY SKILLS

SECTION V

ADMINISTRATION OF PRIMARY EDUCATION

List of Tables

SECTION I

Adult Education Programmes and Performance

1

Evolution of Adult Education: A Historical Perspective

Adult Education has existed in India since time immemorial. The objective of education was to teach a man to be a learned member of his community. In earlier days, literacy had little importance as the real education.[1] Ancient Indian tradition regarded education as the most important for self-realisation. Thus, knowledge or learning was the cornerstone of the ancient Indian educational system, and was sought as the means to the highest end of life, viz. emancipation.[2] Even today, there are numerous religious mendicants who cannot read or write, but who can expound some of the deepest philosophies of the Hindu religion, while others can compose beautiful hymns and sing them. In fine art too, people who can carve on marble or wood make artistic objects without having learned the rudiments of drawing or geometry. Further, illiterate peasants show wonderful knowledge of their religion, agriculture, folklore and epics[3].

Besides, instruction of religious, civic and social branches was given by professional mean called "Kathakas". These 'Kathakas' recited from memory, and sometimes read from books. These 'Kathakas' also rendered discourses on questions pertaining to civic, social and other matters. These recitals were done at night and the whole village turned out to listen to them.

The folklore, legends, ballads, epics, ethical texts and devotional hymns were handed down orally from father to son, from mother to daughter, etc. to the millions of illiterates. The weekly or bi-weekly market was yet another ancient institution in India. The markets were not only centres where people assemble to sell their products and buy their requirements but they were also centres for meeting friends from other villages and for providing recreational facilities.[4]

British Period

The establishment of British rule in India was the main factor responsible for directing India's course of future development. During this period the British intended to completely disregard the indigenous education system and to impart to the people the knowledge of English literature and science through the medium of English language. The English rulers had very little concern for the education of adults. The emergence of night schools in England in the wake of Industrial Revolution had an impact in India. Financial provisions were made for giving grant to night schools in every British Indian province. In view of this development, a commission was appointed in 1882 known as the Indian Education Commission. When the Commission examined thoroughly the functioning of these schools in British Indian provinces it was found that in Bombay there were 134 night schools attended by 3,919 persons in addition to 223 night classes attended by 4,962 persons in the Southern Division of the Presidency. Further, the Commission found that there were over 1,000 night schools in Bengal and 291 night schools in Madras. The Commission (1882-83), in its report submitted to the British government pointed out that such schools had chances of success where the adults needed further education for economic betterment. The Commission as such strongly recommended the extension of the night schools programmes in all the provinces.[5]

With the dawn of the nineteenth century a few countries in the world were able to raise their living standard. India was left far behind in this march of progress. This resulted in unemployment and degeneration of social and cultural life. All these events generated among the Indian middle classes a strong sense of awareness of the situation and the need for social and political change. This awareness gradually developed into two forceful movements, one for social reforms and the other for political revolution.

In 1920, under the leadership of Mahatma Gandhi the struggle for freedom was intensified and took the form of 'mass movement'. After the suspension of the movement in 1922, Gandhiji directed this energy towards organisation of night schools and literacy classes. Thus, there were literacy classes for illiterate adults in cities, towns and villages. National schools and colleges which owed their existence to the mass movement took active part in the literacy work.

With the introduction of diarchy, popular interest in franchise and mass education took place. The co-operative movement which was gaining strength, also provided an invaluable base for starting adult literacy classes. During this period, the most significant development took place in Punjab where in 1925-26 there were 3,206 adult literacy classes with 8,371 pupils.[6]

After the installation of the Congress ministries in provinces in 1937 the constructive programme including literacy campaigns had taken the form of mass movement. The first mass literacy drive was launched in Bihar by setting up a Mass Literacy Committee, consisting of official and non-official members with education minister as chairman. Similar programmes and activities were organised in other provinces as well. For the first time, adult education was accepted as a responsibility of the government and adult literacy as a movement.

In the beginning, the adult education programme meant adult literacy and was limited to 3R's, i.e., teaching people to read, write and to learn the elements of simple arithmetic. Nowhere was there any provision for the maintenance of libraries to help neo-literate adults retain their newly acquired literacy skills and make use of them.[7]

The Central Advisory Board of Education in its fourth meeting held in December 1938 appointed a special committee under the Chairmanship of Dr. Syed Mahmud, an education minister from Bihar, to consider the question of adult education.[8] Dr. Mahmud in his address to the committee identified adult literacy as the chief plank of the adult education movement and declared:

> "No Government can make any appreciable headway with its scheme for the promotion of socio-economic welfare of the people unless the people are prepared to meet the government halfway and offer it responsive cooperation. This responsive cooperation is only feasible when the people possess some amount of education".[9]

But after the outbreak of the World War II, when Congress ministries had to resign, the enthusiasm for adult education and literacy campaigns disappeared. Adult education lost its mass character but gained in status. A number of institutions and agencies continued to work even after the enthusiasm for adult education had subsided. An All India Adult Education Association was formed during this period and made valuable contributions by promoting the cause of adult education.

Independence Period

With the dawn of independence, the concept of adult education has changed. Maulana Abdul Kalam Azad, the first education minister of the country emphasized that adult education should not be limited to 3R's. Maulana wanted that adult education should prepare every citizen to play his part effectively in a democratic social order. Thus, the concept used was 'civic literacy' which was based on life-oriented approach and focused on social education.[10]

Post-Independence Period

The post-independence period in adult education is characterised by the emergence of the concept of social education. The Central Advisory Board of Education, in its meeting held in January 1948, expressed the view that adult education in India had become imperative. To this effect, a committee was appointed under the chairmanship of Shri Mohan Lal Saxena to discuss the matter. The committee in its report submitted to the Government of India, recommended that greater emphasis should be laid on general education to enable every Indian to participate effectively in the new social order. However, the Central Advisory Board of Education in its 15th meeting held at Allahabad in 1949 accepted the Saxena Committee report and recommended social education as the goal for the education of adults.[11]

When the Constitution of India was adopted in 1950, elementary education received much attention. Article 45 of the Constitution of India declared that the State shall endeavour to provide, within a period of ten years from the commencement of this Constitution, free and compulsory education for all children until they attain the age of fourteen years. Soon thereafter, in 1951, India initiated the process of planned development to raise the living standard of its people and open up new opportunities for a richer and varied life. Growth with social justice, modernisation and self-reliance are the key elements of the strategy of development for the purpose. Thus, considering the role of adult education as an instrument of social change and development, social education was launched in the First Five-Year Plan.[12]

In 1952 the concept of civic literacy was modified and was integrated with Community Development Programme. The programme was implemented all over India during the first two Five-Year Plans. It was estimated that nearly 35 lakh illiterates would become literates during the First Five-Year Plan and about 40 lakhs during the Second Plan.

Throughout the 1960s various government committees drew attention to the urgent need to tackle the problem of adult literacy. The most comprehensive committee report was of the Education Commission (1964-66). The appointment of the Education Commission in 1964 under the chairmanship of Dr. D.S. Kothari was one of the most significant events in the history of adult education. The Commission in its report submitted to the Government of India in 1966 recommended a nation-wide campaign to end illiteracy within twenty years. Further, the Commission recommended the setting up of a National Board of Adult Education. On the basis of the Kothari Commission Report, a Parliamentary Committee chaired by the former chairman of Education, Dr. Triguna Sen, drafted a statement on National Policy on Education. After the Parliament discussed the statement, the Indian Government issued a resolution on National Policy on Education incorporating the recommendation of the Kothari Commission.[13]

The resolution on the National Policy on Education adopted in 1968 further declared that the radical reconstruction of education was proposed so that it involved: (i) a transformation of the system to relate it more closely to the life of the people; (ii) a continuous effort to expand educational opportunity; (iii) a sustained effort to raise the quality of education at all stages; (iv) an emphasis on the development of science and technology, and (v) cultivation of moral and social values.[14]

The setting up of the National Board of Adult Education in 1969 and the 1968 National Policy on Education indicates some seriousness on the part of the authorities about adult education programme. Some new programmes like the Farmers' Functional Literacy Project (FFLP) and *Shramik Vidyapiths* (*Jana Shikshan Sansthans*) also received enhanced funding. By 1970s, the concept of development literacy based on Social Change approach came to be evolved. Literacy was described not just as the process of learning the skills of reading, writing and arithmetic but as contribution to the liberation of man and to his full development.[15]

In 1977, the government declared universalisation of adult education and it was given the highest priority. A draft policy statement on adult education was issued and operationalised in the form of the National Adult Education Programme (NAEP). The NAEP was launched on October 2, 1978 with the aim of making an estimated 100 million illiterate persons in the age group of 15-35 years literate over a six-year period (1978-84). Of these, sixty five million persons were to be covered in the Sixth Plan period (1978-83) and the remaining 35 million persons in the first year of the next plan. The programme is a joint and collaborative effort of the Central Government, State governments, Union territory administrations, voluntary agencies, universities, colleges and youth centres. The NAEP is a package which envisages (i) imparting literacy skills to the target illiterate population, (ii) their functional development, and (iii) creation of awareness among them regarding laws and policies of the government for implementation of redistributive justice. Special emphasis was placed on the education of women, scheduled castes and scheduled tribes and other weaker sections of society, comprising the bulk of illiterate population in India.[16]

Unfortunately, the promise of the NAEP was not fulfilled. The Sixth Plan allocated only Rs. 2,000 million against an estimated requirement of Rs. 6,860 million for making 65 million persons literate between 1978 and 1983. In the new government's Sixth Plan (1980 to 1985), plan outlay for adult education was allocated only Rs. 1,280 million as against 2,000 million in the 1978-83 plan. However, a Review Committee appointed in October 1979 found that while the size of adult education programme was 6,75,000 in 1977-78 before the NAEP was launched, it arose only modestly in relation to the target over the next two years. Although the 1979 Review Committee recommended that the programme be strengthened and expanded so that the NAEP should grow into a kind of action programme for development through education and from education through development, but these were not followed up. However, much the same programme was launched afresh in 1982 under the title of 'Adult Education Programme' (AEP) and subsequently given a prominent place in the Programme of Action (1986) based on the Rajiv Gandhi Government's National Policy on Education. It was now rechristened as the National Programme of Adult Education (NPAE). The main aim of the new NPAE is to provide education including literacy to the population in 15-35 age group which numbers about 100 million illiterates.[17]

The Government of India's policy towards adult education has undergone significant changes over the years. In 1985 with the change of government at the centre, an official decision was taken to formulate a new education policy for "reshaping the education system to enable it to meet the challenges of the future".[18] The New Education Policy (NEP) which was finalised in 1986 after a series of consultations and debates at various levels gave a new orientation to adult education in India. Recognising the importance of adult education as a tool for reducing economic, social and gender disparities, the NEP stressed that the "whole nation must pledge itself to the eradication of illiteracy particularly in the 15-35 age group".[19] A New Programme of Action (POA) 1986 was prepared in line with the new education policy, the POA announced a new NPAE which was to be phased, time bound programme covering approximately 40 million by 1990 and another 60 million by 1995. For the first time in the history of Indian adult education, the liquidation of illiteracy was considered as a societal and technology mission.[20]

Two programmes of adult education, the Rural Functional Literacy Programme (RFLP) launched by the Central Government and the *Gram Shikshan Mohim* (Village Literacy Movement) initiated in the State of Maharashtra contributed significantly to the information of the NAEP. Further, a third programme of major dimensions was the Non-Formal Education Scheme launched in 1975-76 for the 15-35 age group. This was to cater especially to young people from the 'weaker sections' who had been denied formal schoolings.[21]

The Rural Functional Literacy Programme (RFLP) is a sub-programme of the Adult Education Programme fully funded by the Central Government and implemented by the States and Union Territories. The broad objectives of the programme are: (i) to develop abilities in the learners about their rights and duties and the benefits they can draw from various schemes of socio-economic development being implemented by the government. The RFLP was launched in May 1986 by involving the NSS and other student volunteers in colleges and universities on the principle of "Each one Teach one". The programme has been designed keeping in view the needs and languages of the learners.

The NPAE was essentially a continuing of the then ongoing schemes of the RFLP, State Adult Education Programmes (SAEP) and the programme of assistance to voluntary agencies. To these was added the Mass Programme of Functional Literacy (MPFL) which envisaged students, educational institutions, trade unions, local bodies and other individual organisations taking up literacy work voluntarily on 'Each one teach one' basis, with provisions of reimbursement for actual field expenses incurred by them.[22]

Subsequently, in 1987, when the Government of India identified eradication of illiteracy as one of the five national missions, the whole machinery of the state became alert and action oriented to the cause of adult education. In accordance with the directives of the National Policy on Education and the implementation strategies envisaged in the POA, the Government of India formulated comprehensive programme and constituted National Literacy Mission (NLM) with a view to achieving literacy goals through setting into motion TLC all over the country in a phased manner. The NLM was launched by Rajiv Gandhi, the then Prime Minister of India on May 5, 1988. The NLM has a time bound objective of imparting functional literacy to 80 million illiterate persons in the age group 15-35 years by 1995. It aims covering 30 million illiterates by 1990 and an additional 50 million illiterates by 1995.[23]

The NLM concept of functional literacy implies: (a) achieving self-reliance in literacy and numeracy, (b) becoming aware of the causes of one's deprivation and moving towards an amelioration of one's condition, through organisation and participation in the process of development, (c) acquiring skills to improve the economic status and general well-being, (d) imbibing values of national integration, conservation of the environment, women's equality, observance of small family norm, etc.[24]

The NLM aims at involving the youth and voluntary agencies in the programme. In addition, *Shramik Vidyapeeths* and 16 State Resource Centres are functioning in different States to cater to the workers' education and to provide technical resource support to the programme.[25] The mission also speaks of efforts to secure people's participation, improve ongoing programmes like the RFLP and the SAEP, expand the mass programme of functional literacy and institutionalise post-literacy and continuing education.

The national level management structure for the NLM called the National Literacy Mission Authority (NLMA) provided for an autonomous body vested with financial and executive powers. The NLMA has a two-tier structure. The Council is headed by the Union Minister for Human Resource Development. The Executive Committee (EC) of the NLMA is headed by the Union Education Secretary. The EC of the NLMA serves as the operational leadership of the mission within the broad parameters of policy enunciated by the council.[26]

Subsequently, few months after launching the NLM, two new developments took place which transformed totally the character and future course of development of the NLM, and of the literacy scenario and outlook in the country. These dramatic developments are the "people's science movement" proposed and implemented by the *Kerala Sastra Sahitya Parishat* (KSSP) and the other by the *Bharat Gyan Vigyan Samithi*. The KSSP came into being formally in the early 1960s, but grew into a mass movement in 1970s and 1980s. By the mid-1980s science organisation had emerged in different parts of the country. Altogether, 26 such organisations came together in 1987.[27]

With the financial assistance and catalytic support from the National Council of Science and Technology Communication (NCSTC) of the Union Government's Department of Science and Technology, these organisations organised the *Bharat Jan Vigyan Jatha* (BJVJ) as a massive communication to promote scientific awareness and temper. The three slogans popularised by the BJVJ were 'Science for the Nation', 'Science for the People' and 'Science for Discovery'. The BJVJ evoked a very positive response all over the country and expand people's science organisations. This also led to the constituent units which together organised the BJVJ coming together in a national network known as the All India People's Science Network (AIPSN).[28]

In February 1988, the Government of India as provided in the NLM document decided to establish *Jana Shikshan Nilayams* (JSNs) all over the country in a phased manner. The intention behind establishing the JSNs was to institutionalise post-literacy and continuing education.[29]

A JSN set up for a cluster of 4-5 villages to cover a population of about 5000 served as the window for securing information on various developmental programmes. The JSN includes programmes being organised as part of farmer's training programmes, rural radio forum and *Charcha Mandals*, youth clubs, *Mahila Mandals*, Mobile and Village Library System, Rural Reading Rooms, etc. A *prerak* being in-charge of JSN one expected that 60,000 JSN would be opened by 1990 and another 60,000 JSNs by 1995. Each JSN is expected to provide a library and a reading room, short duration training programmes relating to health, family welfare, and agriculture and to organise sports, adventure activities, recreational and cultural facilities and evening classes for upgradation of literacy and numeracy skills. Determined efforts are made towards extending it to weaker sections of the society.[30]

In 1989 an extremely significant development took place. It was on January 26, 1989 that the total literacy campaign (TLC) in the Ernakulam district of Kerala was launched. The objective was to make 2,00,000 persons in the district literate within one year through a voluntary based programme. The campaign which was implemented by the KSSP was a collaborative effort of the District Administration and non-governmental organisations. More than 1.5 lakh persons were made literate by 20,000 volunteer instructors. Out of 1.85 lakh, 1.35 lakh learners reached the NLM levels of literacy and numeracy, thus raising the rate of literacy from 77 to 98 per cent. On February 4, 1990 Ernakulam was declared as the first fully literate district in the country.[31]

In the wake of the success of the Ernakulam literacy campaign, similar mass campaign was launched in 1989-90 in the Union Territory of Pondicherry and several districts of West Bengal, Karnataka and Andhra Pradesh as well as in all the remaining districts of Kerala. By April 1991, the *'Akshara Kerelam'* project had been successfully completed making Kerala the first fully literate state in the country.

The TLC model or what we prefer to call, the Mass Literacy Campaign (MLC) model has proved its viability on the ground.

The MLC as the primary strategy to achieve the NLM targets later has become an official policy instrument for eliminating adult illiteracy. The POA 1992 states:

> "After experimenting with successive alternative models of literacy programmes, we have settled down to one which is area-specific, time-bound, voluntary based cost effective outcome oriented. This has given us a lot of hope and faith that illiteracy is not a fatality and can be overcome in a time-bound manner with planned, corrected and co-ordinated effort..."[32]

Identifying universalisation of elementary education, eradication of illiteracy in the age group 15-35 years and strengthening of vocational education as thrust areas, the plan document 1992 further noted 'The changed approach, improved methodology of teaching, increased participation of Non-Governmental Organisations (NGOs) and student volunteers have infused a new vitality into the literacy programme and have given it a fresh momentum."[33]

Finally, the 1992 document lays down the policy and priorities in adult literacy thus:

> Literacy programmes will be launched in districts/regions which are educationally backward or which have a high concentration of scheduled castes, scheduled tribes population or have low female literacy. By the close of the 8th Plan, 345 districts including about two-thirds of all districts in the educationally backward states would be covered by TLC, while the centre-based approach would be gradually phased out and confined to hilly tribal and sparsely populated regions.[34]

Conclusions

The development of adult education in India has to be studied in the light of social forces that have been moulding it during the last one and a half century. During the first three decades after independence India had been able to develop a number of institutions for carrying out educational facilities for its working adults. Since, these have been scattered and uncoordinated; the desired results could not be achieved. The primary problem in eradication of illiteracy is creating motivation and environment for learning and education. Despite efforts at social and economic development since attainment of independence majority of people continue to remain deprived of education, which is one of the basic needs for human development. The adult education programmes have been unsuccessful in the past mainly because the efforts are made to begin with adult literacy. Secondly, the adult literacy is not placed within a wider social context and thirdly, the problem has been viewed more in the context of teaching methods and of learning to read and write. The TLC or what we would prefer to call the MLC has thus proved its viability on the ground.

Over and above, adult education programme is being implemented largely through the centrally sponsored scheme. For attaining of total literacy, government alone cannot solve the vast problem of illiteracy. The efforts of the government will, therefore, have to be supplemented and strengthened by voluntary organisations and individuals who have a positive perception and commitment.

NOTES

1. S.S. Bhat, *Growth and Development of Adult Education*, New Delhi, 1992, pp. 13-14.
2. A.L. Rahi, *Adult Education Policies and Programmes*, Ambala Cantt., 1996, pp. 13-14.
3. S.S. Bhat, *Growth and Development of Adult Education*, New Delhi, 1992, p. 14.
4. *Ibid.*, pp. 14-15.
5. *Ibid.*, p. 15.
6. A.L. Rahi, *Adult Education Policies and Programme*, Ambala Cantt., 1996, p. 17.
7. *Ibid.*, p. 18.
8. Report by the Central Advisory Board of Education, January 1944 Post-War Educational Development in India, Ministry of Education, Government of India, Delhi, 1964, p. 68.

9. F.N. 3, p. 15.
10. *Ibid.*, p. 5.
11. *Ibid.*, p. 17.
12. A.B. Venkatesh and C.R. Sheela, *Literacy and Empowerment*, New Delhi, 1996, pp. 69-70.
13. *Ibid.*, pp. 72-73.
14. Seventh Five-Year Plan (1985-90), Vol. II. Government of India, Planning Commission, p. 252.
15. A.B. Venkatesh, C.R. Sheela, *op. cit.*, pp. 73-74.
16. M.L. Mehta, Adult Education and Total Development in the *Journal of Social Change*: June 1989: Vol. 19, No. 2, pp. 25-27.
17. F.N. 2, pp. 84-85.
18. Government of India, *Challenges of Education—A Policy Perspective*, New Delhi: Ministry of Education, 1985.
19. Government of India, *National Policy on Education*, 1986, New Delhi: Ministry of Human Resource Development, 1986, p. 9.
20. *Government of India Programme of Action*, New Delhi, Ministry of Human Resource Development, 1986, p. 136.
21. F.N. 12, p. 75.
22. *Ibid.*, pp. 87-90
23. Government of India, *National Literacy Mission*, New Delhi, Directorate of Adult Education, Government of India Press, New Delhi.
24. *Ibid.*
25. *Ibid.*
26. F.N.12, pp. 91-92.
27. F.N.12, p. 94.
28. *Ibid.*
29. S.S. Bhatt., *Growth and Development of Adult Education*, Cosmo Publication, New Delhi, 1992, pp. 32-33.
30. Government of India, Books for Post-Literacy Guidelines, Directorate of Adult Education, New Delhi, p. 13 and pp. 25-26; Government of India, *National Literacy Mission*, Directorate of Adult Education, Ministry of Human Resource Developments.
31. F.N. 12, p. 33
32. *Ibid.*, p. 97
33. *Ibid.*
34. *Ibid.*, pp. 98-99.

2

Illiteracy: Impact and Problems

Officially, the International Literacy Year (ILY) was launched on 6 December, 1989 at the United Nations Headquarters in New York (United States). On this occasion, the United Nations Secretary General, Javier Perez de Cuellar, stated "Illiteracy is a concern to the United Nations because for nearly one billion men and women, the illiterate adults of the world, the right to education proclaimed in the Universal Declaration of Human Rights is rhetoric." The Director-General of UNESCO, Federico Mayor, struck an optimistic note by declaring that 'the rate of illiteracy in the adult population had declined from an estimated 40 per cent in 1960 to 28 per cent in 1990. For the first time the absolute number of illiterates put at 965 million has begun to decline. It was because of this crucial problem that the United Nations had declared the year 1990 as the International Literacy Year for launching the Plan of Action for the eradication of illiteracy by the year 2000. The objective was to generate public awareness about the importance to the progress of literacy, such as reducing primary school drop-outs and establishing post-literacy programmes to prevent relapse into illiteracy[1].

At the national level, the ILY was launched by the Prime Minister of India at New Delhi on January 22, 1990. At this functions student and non-student volunteers were asked to muster their collective strength in spreading the message of literacy as well as imparting of literacy.

In 1991, the Census Commission of India defined literacy as 'literate' any person who can read and write "with understanding", in any Indian language, and not merely read and write. Those who can read but cannot write are not literate. Formal education in a school is not necessary for a person to be considered as literate. Literacy as defined by UNESCO is one who can with understanding both read and write a short simple statement relevant to his everyday life. Literacy is not the simple reading of word or a set of associated symbols and sounds, but an act of critical understanding of men's situation in the world.

The National Policy of Education, 1986 popularly known as the New Education Policy was first given by the Prime Minister of India in his first broadcast to the nation on January 5, 1985. The need for the new policy arose from the fact that the implementation of the 1968 was incomplete and uneven. No plans of action were prepared for its implementation nor adequate funds were made available for the purpose. The number of illiterates increased and the standards decline considerably. New technologies emerged and changes occurred everywhere. The New Education Policy was designed to see that a national system of education is created and all imbalances and disparities are removed in all sectors of education. The New Education Policy gives the highest priority to solving the problem of children dropping out of school all over the country. The new policy ensured that all children who attain the age of 11 years by 1990 will have had five years of schooling. Likewise, by 1995 all children will be provided free and compulsory education up to 14 years of age. This New Education Policy makes it clear that the non-formal education is in no way inferior to formal school education[2].

India has made considerable progress since independence in terms of increase in all types of institutions, enrolment and diversification of educational programmes. The number of recognized educational institutions has increase more than three times. It has increased from 2.31 lakhs in 1951 to 7.55 lakhs in 1985. The enrolment of students in the educational institutions has increased more than five times, that is, from 24 million to 132 million in the same period. An increase in the total number of literates has also been registered[3]. It increases from 16.7 per cent in 1951 to 65.38 per cent in 2001.

The table below will show the percentage of literacy in India from 1901 to 2001.

Table 2.1: All India Literacy Rates 1901-2001

Year	*Population*	*Illiterates*	*Literates*	*Literacy Rate*	*Percentage*	*Total*
1901	235.1	222.5	12.6	9.8	0.6	5.3
1911	248.2	233.5	14.7	10.6	1.1	5.9
1921	246.7	229.0	17.7	12.2	1.8	7.2
1931	273.4	247.4	26.0	15.6	2.9	9.5
1941	312.0	261.8	50.2	24.9	7.3	16.1
1951	353.1	294.2	58.9	25.0	7.9	16.7
1961	428.0	325.5	102.6	34.4	13.0	24.0
1971	533.5	376.2	157.3	39.5	18.7	29.4
1981	665.3	424.3	241.0	46.9	24.8	36.2
1991	843.9	481.9	362.0	63.8	39.4	52.11
2001	1027.0	300.14	866.87	75.85	54.16	65.38

Source: Census of India, 2001.

Scope and Magnitude of Illiteracy

Illiteracy is one of the major causes of backwardness and the root cause of exploitation. In an Indian village, illiteracy keeps people change to ignorance, inaction and exploitation in a number of ways. For instance, a villager might refuse primary medical care for his family while putting his faith in some faith healer's. The eradication of illiteracy by the year 2000 is a challenge that it cannot be met by UNESCO's action alone, particularly since such action does not produce its impact directly. The search for illiterates is one of the biggest and most crucial event of this century. Ever since independence, the Government of India has been emphasizing more on primary education for all. When the planning process started in 1951, 18.33 per cent of the population could claim knowledge of an alphabet or numbers. The rate had gone up to 28.30 per cent in 1961; 34.45 per cent in 1971; 43.57 per cent in 1981. As per 2001 Census, 300.14 million are illiterate, comprising 29.4 per cent of the total non-literates in the world. The current policy of National Literacy Mission (NLM) has fixed the target of achieving 75 per cent literacy by 2005, but the Tenth Five Year Plan has extended it to 2007. The Darker Framework of Education for All has set the target of achieving 50 per cent improvement in levels of adult literacy by 2.15[4]. Even after more than six decades of independence, India is still lagging behind from this constitutional obligation. India is the largest producer of graduates in the world. With the advancement of science and technologies, space research etc., there had been tremendous strides in agricultural and food production. Despite such advancement and progress, India, as per the 2001 Census, had 300.14 million illiterates (seven plus age-group)[5]. Today, 58 years after India achieved Independence, it is found that majority of the illiterates in the world are Indians. Out of every 20 people in the world, three are Indians, of whom two are illiterates. Five out of every ten Indians, three out of every five women and eight out of ten scheduled castes and scheduled tribes still cannot read and write[6]. Further, out of every 100 children who enrolled in class one, only 25 reached class six and the number declined further in the educational ladder. Of the total illiterate people, about 100 million illiterates belong to the age-group of 15-35 years which is considered to be the most productive age, crucial to the task of national reconstruction[7].

With regard to the literacy percentage in India as a whole the following tables highlights a high literacy rate of some State and Union Territory.

Table 2.2: High Literacy Rate (80 per cent and above)

Sl.No.	*State/Union Territory*	*Total*	*Male*	*Female*
1.	Kerela	90.92	94.20	87.86
2.	Mizoram	88.49	90.69	86.13
3.	Lakshadweep	87.52	93.15	81.56
4.	Goa	82.32	88.88	75.51
5.	Delhi	81.82	87.37	75.00
6.	Chandigarh	81.76	85.65	76.65
7.	Pondicherry	81.49	88.89	74.13
8.	Andaman & Nicobar Islands	81.18	86.07	75.29
9.	Daman & Diu	81.09	88.40	70.37

Source: Census of India 2001—Final Figures

In terms of all India ranking in literacy rate, the following table highlights the literacy rate of states above national average (65.4%) and below 80 per cent.

Table 2.3: Literacy Rate of States above National Average

(in Percentage)

Sl.No.	*State/Union Territory*	*Total*	*Male*	*Female*
1.	Maharashtra	77.27	86.27	67.51
2.	Himachal Pradesh	77.13	86.02	68.08
3.	Tripura	73.66	81.47	65.41
4.	Tamil Nadu	73.47	82.33	64.55
5.	Uttaranchal	72.28	84.01	60.26
6.	Gujarat	69.97	80.50	58.60
7.	Punjab	69.95	75.63	63.55
8.	Sikkim	69.68	76.73	61.46
9.	West Bengal	69.22	77.58	60.22
10.	Manipur	68.87	77.87	59.70
11.	Haryana	68.59	79.25	56.31
12.	Nagaland	67.11	71.77	61.92
13.	Karnataka	67.04	76.29	57.45

Source: Census of India 2001—Final Figures.

In terms of the lowest literacy rate, the following table highlights the literacy rate of States below national average (65.4%).

Table 2.4: Literacy Rate of States below National Average

(in percentage)

Sl.No.	*State/Union Territory*	*Total*	*Male*	*Female*
1.	Chattisgarh	65.18	77.86	52.40
2.	Assam	64.28	71.93	56.03
3.	Madhya Pradesh	64.11	76.80	50.28
4.	Orissa	63.61	75.95	50.97
5.	Meghalaya	63.31	66.14	60.41
6.	Andhra Pradesh	61.11	70.85	51.17
7.	Rajasthan	61.03	76.46	44.34
8.	Dadra & Nagar Haveli	60.03	73.32	42.99
9.	Uttar Pradesh	57.36	70.23	42.98
10.	Arunachal Pradesh	54.74	64.07	44.24
11.	Jammu & Kashmir	54.46	65.75	41.82
12.	Jharkhand	54.13	67.94	39.38
13.	Bihar	47.53	60.32	33.57

Source: Census of India 2001—Final Figures.

Table 2.5: Expenditure on Education (1951 to 1998)

(*Rs. in millions*)

Year	*Total Exp. on Edn. & Trg. (Rev.)*	*Total Exp. on Adult Edn.*	*Total Exp on all sectors (Rev.)*	*GDP*	*% of Ednl. exp. to all sectors exp.*	*% of Ednl. exp. to GDP*	*% of adult exp. to all sectors*	*% of adult edn. to GDP*	*% of adult edn. to total exp. on edn.*
1951	644.6	34.17	8141.30	94450	7.92	0.68	0.42	0.04	5.30
1952	722.6	35.79	8576.7	93240	8.43	0.77	0.42	0.04	4.95
1953	800.6	34.61	9082	101610	8.82	0.79	0.38	0.03	4.32
1954	958.2	35.91	9737.40	95340	9.84	1.01	0.37	0.04	3.75
1955	1183.9	38.29	11112.6	97070	10.65	1.22	0.34	0.04	3.23
1956	1328.8	46.19	11580.1	115830	11.47	1.15	0.40	0.04	3.48
1957	1502.6	67.16	14166.2	118390	10.61	1.27	0.47	0.06	4.47
1958	1737.8	84.14	15943.6	132310	10.9	1.31	0.53	0.06	4.84
1959	2075.9	93.76	17700.6	138770	11.73	1.5	0.53	0.07	4.52
1960	2395.6	120.15	19979.3	151820	11.99	1.58	0.60	0.08	5.02
1961	2603	129.57	22254	159990	11.7	1.63	0.58	0.08	4.98
1962	2787.6	137.24	29426.7	171040	9.47	1.63	0.47	0.08	4.92
1963	3139.3	151.88	34889.7	195590	9	1.61	0.44	0.08	4.84
1964	3692.9	129.47	38449.1	228360	9.6	1.62	0.34	0.06	3.51
1965	4326.1	131.26	44048.2	238990	9.82	1.81	0.30	0.05	3.03
1966	4878.3	144.74	51002.4	271590	9.56	1.8	0.28	0.05	2.97
1967	5931.4	160.00	56197.7	319290	10.55	1.86	0.28	0.05	2.70

(*Contd.*)

Table 2.5 (Contd.)

1968	6491.3	166.40	69220.7	336880	9.38	1.93	0.24	0.05	2.56
1969	7602.3	179.21	79080.7	370570	9.61	2.05	0.23	0.05	2.36
1970	8923.6	198.86	87871.2	394240	10.16	2.26	0.23	0.05	2.23
1971	10110.7	202.00	106109	419570	9.53	2.41	0.19	0.05	2.00
1972	11504.3	88.72	118636	461710	9.78	2.49	0.07	0.02	0.77
1973	13007.2	136.64	128845	566290	10.1	2.3	0.11	0.02	1.05
1974	15706.7	122.90	146250	667480	10.74	2.35	0.08	0.02	0.78
1975	18494.7	147.95	179590	709460	10.3	2.61	0.08	0.02	0.80
1976	20390.9	166.66	204828	763030	9.96	2.67	0.08	0.02	0.82
1977	26306	87.24	226663	871180	11.61	3.02	0.04	0.01	0.33
1978	29946.9	130.92	261348	937240	11.46	3.2	0.05	0.01	0.44
1979	33475.7	373.02	309154	1025950	10.83	3.26	0.12	0.04	1.11
1980	38841.9	253.70	363984	1227720	10.67	3.16	0.07	0.02	0.65
1981	44359	298.6	336673	1432560	10.30	3.00	0.09	0.02	0.67
1982	57363.2	374.74	439962	1587610	13.18	3.47	0.09	0.02	0.65
1983	62295.3	533.71	618893	1857790	13.04	3.35	0.09	0.03	0.86
1984	74558.8	464.57	690255	2071090	10.8	3.6	0.07	0.02	0.62
1985	87130.2	875.83	670914	2323700	12.99	3.75	0.13	0.04	1.01
1986	94791.3	1012.03	804547	2582250	11.78	3.67	0.13	0.04	1.07
1987	117983.5	1346.11	925184	2922320	12.75	4.04	0.15	0.05	1.14
1988	140698.2	1945.59	1075438	3490210	13.08	4.03	0.18	0.06	1.38
1989	179500	2134.88	1260460	4086620	14.24	4.39	0.17	0.05	1.19
1990	204910	2731.47	1467115	4778140	13.97	4.29	0.19	0.06	1.33

(Contd.)

Table 2.5 (Contd.)

Year	*Total Exp. on Edn. & Trg. (Rev.)*	*Total Exp. on Adult Edn.*	*Total Exp on all sectors (Rev.)*	*GDP*	*% of Ednl. exp. to all sectors exp.*	*% of Ednl. exp. to GDP*	*% of adult exp. to all sectors*	*% of adult edn. to GDP*	*% of adult edn. to total exp. on edn.*
1991	223490	2285.08	1703704	5892730	13.14	3.79	0.13	0.04	1.02
1992	250300	2455.47	1903275	6307720	13.15	3.97	0.13	0.04	0.98
1993	282800	3248.27	2185352	7813450	12.94	3.62	0.15	0.04	1.15
1994	326060	3383.13	2516919	8680190	12.95	3.76	0.13	0.04	1.04
1995	381780	2597.15	2861946	10732710	13.34	3.55	0.09	0.02	0.68
1996	438960	2057.45	3293899	12435460	13.33	3.52	0.06	0.02	0.47
1997	519310	2098.01	3807285	13900420	13.64	3.73	0.06	0.02	0.40
1998	608570	1894.47	4416225	16160330	13.7[illegible]	3.77	0.04	0.01	0.31

Source: S.Y. Shah., Financing of Adult Education in India, (n.d.), pp. 27-28.

Although the literacy rate in India has increased from 52.21 per cent in 1991 to 64.84 per cent in 2001 showing an increase of 12.63 per cent, yet in absolute terms, the number of illiterates has increased from 29.42 crore in 1951 to 300.14 million in 2001. This percentage reveals that India produce large number of illiterates' people in the world.

India's record on spending for education is pathetic. The total expenditure on education for the period during 1980-81 to 1990-91, as a percentage of gross domestic product (GDP) has covered between 2.8 and 3.8 per cent. It was stagnant at around 3 per cent during the early eighties, but has improved marginally since 1987-88. But as a percentage of total government expenditure, expenditure on education declined from 13 per cent in 1982-83 to 11.1 per cent in 1990-91. In contrast other developing countries like China spend 25.7 per cent and Kenya 21.5 per cent on education much more than India[8]. Table 2.6 shows the details expenditure of India on education from 1951 to 1998.

As regards the share of education, the total plan outlay in the share of education has declined from 7.9 per cent during the First Plan period to 3.6 per cent in the Seventh Plan. The expenditure on higher education has shown a sharp rise from 9 per cent in the First Plan to 25 per cent in the Fourth Plan and to 14 per cent in the Seventh Plan. The increase in the share of higher education has been at the expense of primary education whose share fell from 56 per cent in the First Plan to only 29 per cent in the Seventh Plan[9].

Notwithstanding the enormous expansion of adult education, the problem of illiteracy has been lingering on. Though in terms of population, India is the second largest country in the world with 1027 million people as per 2001 census, it has the highest number of illiterates with 300 million illiterates, forming 29.2 per cent of total illiterates in the world. The problem becomes more acute due to 29.9 per cent of people living below the poverty line and wide gender and regional disparities. Over the years, there was not only an increase in the percentage of literacy, but also the number of literates increased by more than ten times during 1951-2001, i.e. from 55 million to 567 million. While the male literacy increased from

Table 2.6: Expenditure on Adult Education as Percentage of Total Budgeted Expenditure of Central and State Governments (Plan amd Non-Plan) (Revenue Account)

Year	*Centre*			*States*			*Total*		
	Exp. on Adult Edn.	*Total Budgeted Exp.*	%age	Exp. on Adult Edn.	Total Budgeted Exp.	%age	Exp. on Adult Edn.	Total Budgeted Exp.	%age
1951-52	1.71	4048	0.04	32.45	4093	0.79	34.17	8141	0.42
1961-62	2.36	10515	0.02	127.21	11739	1.08	129.57	22254	0.58
1971-72*	22.80	60683	0.04	113.84	45426	0.25	136.64	106109	0.13
1981-82	102.00	239964	0.04	196.60	177193	0.11	298.60	417157	0.07
1986-87	454.10	410861	0.11	557.93	393685	0.14	1012.03	670914	0.15
1991-92	1039.76	823080	0.13	1245.31	880624	0.14	2285.07	1703704	0.13
1996-97	885.60	1589330	0.05	1171.85	1704569	0.07	2057.45	3293899	0.06
1999-2000	826.40	1823500	0.05	1358.52	1884885	0.06	2184.92	3708385	0.06

*Data for year 1971-72 not available, adopted 1973-74 data

Source: S.Y. Shah., Financing of Adult Education in India, (n.d.), p. 25.

Table 2.7: State-wise Percentage of Female Literacy in the Country as per 2001 Census

Sl. No.	*Name of the State*	*Percentage of Female Literacy*
1.	Andhra Pradesh	51.17
2.	Arunachal Pradesh	44.24
3.	Assam	56.03
4.	Bihar	33.57
5.	Chattisgarh	52.40
6.	Delhi	75.00
7.	Goa	75.51
8.	Gujarat	58.60
9.	Haryana	56.31
10.	Himachal Pradesh	68.08
11.	Jammu and Kashmir	41.82
12.	Jharkhand	39.38
13.	Karnataka	57.45
14.	Kerela	87.86
15.	Madhya Pradesh	50.28
16.	Maharashtra	67.51
17	Manipur	59.70
18.	Meghalaya	60.41
19.	Mizoram	86.13
20.	Nagaland	61.92
21.	Orissa	50.97
22.	Punjab	63.55
23.	Rajasthan	44.34
24.	Sikkim	61.46
25.	Tamil Nadu	64.55
26.	Tripura	65.41
27.	Uttaranchal	60.26
28.	Uttar Pradesh	42.98
29.	West Bengal	60.22
Union Territories		
1.	Andaman and Nicobar Islands	75.29
2.	Chandigarh	76.65
3.	Dadra and Nagar Haveli	42.99
4.	Daman and Diu	70.37
5.	Lakshadweep	81.56
6.	Pondicherry	74.16
	All India	54.16

Source: Census of India—2001 provisional figures.

64.13 to 75.85 per cent during 1991-2001, the female literacy rate increased from 39.29 to 54.16 per cent in the same period. It is noticed that the female literacy rate during the period 1991-2001 increased by 14.87 per cent whereas male literacy rate rose by 11.72 per cent. Hence the female literacy rate increased by 3.15 per cent more compared to male literacy rate. The table 2.7 will shows the percentage of female literacy in the country as per 2001 census.

Measures adopted for Eradicating Illiteracy

Broadly speaking, four measures have been adopted for the eradication of illiteracy in India. These are as follows:

(i) National Adult Education Programme (NAEP)

The National Adult Education Programme was launched on October 2, 1978 with the aim of providing education and imparting literacy and numeracy skills among all illiterate persons particularly in the age-group of 15-35 years. The programme also aim at promoting functional skills to enable the illiterate to become more productive and to create consciousness about their socio-economic status, policies and programmes of the government to enable them to derive optimum benefits from these programmes[10]. The programme is a joint and collaborative effort of the Central and State Governments, Voluntary agencies, Universities, Colleges and Youth Centre. However, special emphasis is being placed on the education of women, Scheduled Castes and Scheduled Tribes and other weaker sections of the society, who constitute the bulk of illiterate population in India.

(ii) Rural Functional Literacy Programme (RFLP)

The Rural Functional Literacy Programme is a sub-programme of the Adult Education programme which is funded by the Central Government and implemented by the States and Union Territories. The main objectives of this programme are to develop abilities in the learners to read and write, and to create awareness among the learners about their rights and duties and to derive benefits from various schemes of socio-economic development being implemented by the government.

The Rural Functional Literacy Programme was launched in May 1986, by involving the NSS and Student Volunteers in Colleges and Universities on the principle of "Each One Teach One". Starting on a modest scale of two lakh volunteers, it has gone up to 4.50 lakhs in 1990 covering over 4.20 lakhs learners. During 1987 an ambitious programme was adopted involving both students and teachers of schools and colleges with input for research studies on the success of the programme. The programme has been designed keeping in view the needs and languages of the learners. The government has selected 40 districts to improve the quality of adult education[11]. It was only after evaluation of the impact that the programme had taken up in a big way to spread literacy in the minimum possible time.

Meantime, the process of the Mass Programme of Functional Literacy (MPFL) involves various stages. These stages are—selecting masters trainers who are to train the student volunteers; selecting, motivating and mobilizing the literacy work; identifying literate persons in the age group 15-35 who may be staying in the neighbourhood of an educational institution; forging a link between the student volunteers and the illiterate persons and assigning an area of operation for each volunteer; monitoring the programme of the student volunteers by senior teachers and headmasters of schools; co-ordination with various development departments/ agencies by way of visits or functionaries to the place where the volunteer is imparting literacy, telling the learners about the advantages of being literate, making available charts, posters and other materials to the learners; identifying genuine difficulties of the learners; and providing post-literacy activities for the non-literates through libraries and reading rooms. Coverage and support by the media and evaluation of the overall impact of the programme through University Department of Adult and Continuing Education is of crucial importance[12].

(iii) National Literacy Mission (NLM)

In accordance with the directives of the National Policy on Education and the implementation strategies envisaged in the programme of Action, the Government of India formulated a comprehensive programme known as the National Literacy Programme in the field of adult education. The NLM was launched by Late Prime Minister, Rajiv Gandhi on May 5, 1988, to give the literacy programme the much needed prestige and publicity. The NLM has a time bound objective of imparting functional literacy to 80 million illiterate persons in the age-group of 15-35 years—30 million illiterates by 1990 and an additional 50 million by 1995. The Mission, thus, aimed at achieving 80.0 per cent literacy in 1995 in comparison to 36.0 per cent in 1981. The thrust of the Mission will be on women and rural illiterate because 62.7 per cent of the illiterates are women and 85.5 per cent illiterates belong to rural areas. The Mission approach is based on certain assumptions. The first assumption that there would be continuance of political will at all levels for the achievement of mission goals. The second assumption that a national consensus would be created for mobilization of social forces and the third assumption revolves around seeking the participation of people in the Mission. The NLM aimed at involving the youth and voluntary agencies in the programme[13]. In 1990, there were 513 projects in operation in various states and union territories in India. At present, more than 500 Voluntary Agencies are working in the field. In addition, Shramik Vidyapeeths and 16 State Resource Centres are functioning in different States to cater to the workers' education and to provide technical resource support to the programme. The Bharat Gyan Vigyan Jathan (BGVJ) was one such sincere attempt at awakening the conscience of the masses. It was a country-wide campaign by teachers, students, women, youth, creative thinkers, writers, artistes, social and educational activities, undertaken from October 2, 1990 to November 14, 1990 with a view to motivate the whole society towards literacy as part of the NLM.

(iv) Total Literacy Campaign (TLC)

The Centre Base Approach which was the approach under the NAEP and in the earlier phase of the NLM has been replaced with total literacy campaign (TLC). This means total eradication of illiteracy from a compact area. The TLC started in Kottayam town in Kerala. The NSS Volunteers of Mahatma Gandhi University and the Kottayam Municipality joined hands to make Kottayam the fully literate town in 100 days. 2209 persons were to be made literate. The Ministry of Human Resource Development sanctioned 32 NSS Volunteers to work on a full time basis in the 32 Municipal wards of the town. The method was 'each one teaches one'.

The Salient Features of the TLC are: Area specific, time bound, volunteer based and result oriented. Its implementation is through the autonomous registered society under the leadership of a Chief Executive Officer. Under the TLC literacy is created through intensified environment building programme. All kinds of media and art forms are utilized for dissemination of the message that literacy is desirable. TLC depends on voluntarism. This implies that a large number of functionaries on their own will contribute their time, energy and resources to the campaign without any expectation of reward or incentive. Every learner enrolled in the campaign is expected to achieve certain pre-determined levels of literacy and numeracy at the end of the campaign. Thus, a new pedagogy known as Improved Pace and Content of Learning (IPCL) has been developed in the form of three booklets to be completed for about six months.

The TLC is based on the assumption that there would be active involvement of the community and the persons who are expected to benefit from the literacy campaign[14].

University Involvement in Adult Education

Since 1970s every effort has been made to involve the Universities on adult education in a big way. Universities as the institutions of higher learning have been viewed to become adult education agencies. The Indian Adult Education Association had for several years made attempt to persuade the UGC and the Government of India to recognize the responsibility of the universities towards the community. However, it was only the launching of the NAEP in 1978 by the Government of India that provided an opportunity to universities to actively involve themselves with the eradication of illiteracy.

The objective of the literacy programme of the UGC through the universities and colleges were:

(1) Actively involving teachers and students in the universities and colleges in the process of national development through extension programmes for enriching the knowledge and experience of the teachers and students and also for developing the potential of local human resource so that they effectively participate in the development process.
(2) To achieve total literacy in the areas for which the universities and colleges assume responsibility.
(3) To increase the knowledge and awareness to improve the functional skills of the local population in areas which affect their course and quality of life.

Tapping the Student Power

Using the students in literacy campaign is tapping the student power for pulling country out of its stagnation. However, the largest chunk of illiterates in India is in the Hindi belt that is Bihar, Rajasthan, Uttar Pradesh, Andhra Pradesh, Madhya Pradesh, Haryana and Himachal Pradesh. In these States, more than 80 per cent of adults are illiterate. If students' services are used during the vacations in these States the students can effectively utilized for adult education work. The programme has to be time bound and it should be low cost. Students have to devote 2-3 hours a day for two months in teaching the illiterates. The motivation for the student instructors has to come in the form of weightage in passing examination and in getting admissions in education institutions. By this, it enables the students to carry the torch of literacy to millions of illiterate adults, if responsibility is given with a feeling of trust and confidence.

Efforts by Voluntary Organization

Government alone cannot solve the problem of illiteracy in the country. It is also not possible to achieve the objective of total eradication of illiteracy entirely through governmental efforts. The efforts of both the Central and State Governments, therefore, will have to be supplemented and strengthened by Voluntary Organizations and individuals who have a positive perception and commitment. Voluntary Organization can play an important role in eradicating illiteracy as they are aware of the grasroots realities and nearer to the community. VOs can contribute both in creating environment and teaching of illiterates. They can also provide support in providing reading materials for the neo-literates.

Conclusion

Many attempts were made by the Government of India in the past for eradicating illiteracy but it could not succeed because the country was facing various other problems like employment, food and self-reliance. On the other hand, due to the increase in population the number of illiterates progressively increase. In reality, functional literacy programme was expected to lower the rate of infant mortality, reduces the number of school drop-outs, improve health and create awareness etc., but nothing have been able to make good of the problem. The main reason is because Adult Education movement does not have the support from the grassroots. If adult literacy is necessary, a child's education is an urgent national priority. While many State Governments claim to have enacted compulsory primary education, in practice, no state has implemented such a law, to compel school attendance. In fact, instead of talking compulsory education, the decision-makers now talk of universal education. However, it may be concluded that the task of making cent per cent people literate, and persuading the parents of millions of children between 6-14 age-group to send their children to schools required tremendous efforts and a high degree of motivation on the part of learners and the instructors. Such a serious problem of illiteracy calls for drastic measures rather than half-hearted approaches. Mass illiteracy and child education have to be tackled on a war footing because of the sheer magnitude of the illiteracy problem.

NOTES

1. UNESCO Adult Education, *International Literacy Year*, Published by the Family Planning Association of India, Bombay, (n.d), p. 1.
2. Ministry of I & B, Government of India, *National Policy on Education*, (Coronation Litho Work, Sivakasi, December 1987), pp. 1-5.
3. "Literacy Population Nexus", published by the Family Planning Association of India, Bombay, (n.d), p. 2.
4. Shah, S.Y., Financing of Adult Education in India (n.d.), p. 1.
5. See "India on the threshold of Wiping out illiteracy", *Meghalaya Guardian*, (Guwahati), dated January 24, 1994, p. 3.
6. *Mass Campaign for Literacy* (n.d).
7. *Meghalaya Guardian, op. cit.*, dated January 24, 1994, p. 3.
8. *Business India*, (New Delhi), dated May 13-26, 1991, p. 2.
9. *Ibid.*
10. *Indian Journal of Adult Education*, Vol. 47, No. 4, dated April 1986, pp. 15-17.
11. Government of India, *National Literacy Mission*, Ministry of Human Resource Development, New Delhi, 1988.
12. Government of India, *National Literacy Mission: Mass Programme of Functional Literacy (Guidelines)*, Ministry of Human Resource Development, Department of Education, Government of India, New Delhi (n.d.), pp. 1-13.
13. Shah, S.Y., "National Literacy Mission (1988) A Review", *University News*, Vol. XXXVI, No. 36, dated September 5, 1988, pp. 1-2.
14. Sachdeva, J.L., North-East Zone Conference on Adult Education, Shillong, Meghalaya, June 22-23, 1992, *Working Paper*, pp. 3-4.

3

Women Literacy and Total Development

Introduction

Literacy like education means better quality of life, increased productivity and earnings. Literacy is not only an instrument of development, but an investment for progress balanced and equitable socio-economic development. The question what is 'literacy' or why literacy, has been answered time and again. Even then some people have not been able to appreciate the role and value of literacy in the total development effort. They think literacy is limited to the acquisition of the 3R's. They simply forget that literacy has a wider connotation as well and lack of it. That means, illiteracy can seriously affect the personality of an individual and that of a nation.

Literacy is really a key which opens the doors to a wider world—the world of education. One lifetime is not enough to acquire all the knowledge existing in this world. It is because of this that literacy should not be understood simply acquiring the 3R's to read, to write and to perform simple arithmetic. Illiteracy remains a major factor and impediment to the development and well-being of a woman. While the national literacy rate in India is dismal, the female literacy rate is a tragedy. It is more than 32.42 per cent while the male literacy rate is 63.86 per cent; an increase of 13.23 per cent and 32.50 per cent respectively between 1981 and 1991. In absolute terms the number of female illiterates increased by 16.3 million as against 15.8 million in the case of males. In 1991, it is estimated that there are 247.6 million illiterate women in India. The percentage of illiteracy among females today is more than 60.58 per cent in comparison to 36.14 per cent among males. In urban areas, female illiteracy is 52.0 per cent as against 34 per cent among males. In rural areas the rate is 82 per cent as against 59 per cent among males.

Women and Literacy

Literacy is an end in itself as well as a means to an end. The literate women become armed with information and thus are able to fight for their rights. They are able to know more about their children's illness and their treatment. They will also know more about nutrition, health and hygiene. The 1991 census reveal that female literacy has brought down birth rate, death rate and infant mortality rates. Kerala, Goa, Tamil Nadu, Himachal Pradesh, Orissa, Punjab, Karnataka and Gujarat where female literacy has shown upward trends, population growth rate is below 2.0 per cent.

Female literacy has a strong effect on total fertility rate as literate women tend to marry later than illiterate women. Literate women are more likely to enroll their children in school and make better use of the family planning and child and mother care services. Improvement in female literacy has direct effect on reducing fertility. Lower child mortality contribute to lower fertility rate. One of the main reasons why Kerala leads in low birth and low death rates is because of the high level of female literacy. The labour value of children is very high in illiterate households which are generally poorer and need the income of the child. A very large number of girls are yoked to house work or daily wage labour even before they are adults. Girls who attend school in their childhood are pulled out after a year or two. Whatever they learnt in school is forgotten once they leave the school. The one or two years of schooling they received goes waste. Between 1961 and 1981 roughly five million child labours joined the ranks of illiterates every year which comes to 437 million in 1981. Considering only those seven years of age and above, the number of illiterates stood at 302 million in 1981 and 324 million in 1991. The census shows that women in India lack in literacy. While 63.86 per cent of Indian men are literate, only 39.5 per cent of women in India can read and write. Literate women are more knowledgeable about health and hygiene. As a result, most of their children survive which, in turn, reduces the family size. Literate women are also more likely to have work interests outside the family and hence the motivation for fewer children. Female literacy affects fertility not only directly but also indirectly through child mortality and mean age at first marriage. Age of women at marriage are closely related to the infant mortality rate. In India 57.1 per cent of women under 20 years of age are married. Of the 25 million children born everywhere in India, two million children die before reaching the age of one. Majority of these deaths were due to avoidable infections and malnutrition. According to 1991 census India places Infant Mortality Rate (IMR) at 79 and the under five mortality rate at 124 per 1,000 live births. In India IMR ranged from 17 per 1,000 live births in Kerala to 114 in Orissa. The main problem of infant mortality was due to lack of cleanliness, balanced diet, health education especially of mothers, ante-natal care, skilled care at delivery and general ignorance. Most of the Indian women are exposed to pregnancy almost from puberty onwards for a much longer number of years. Education thus pushes up the female mean age at marriage. The higher the female mean age at marriage, the lower the IMR. Child marriages have been very common in India. Of the four million marriages which take place in India in a year, three million are of girls who are under the legal age of 18. As a result, child birth leads to higher rate of maternal mortality and morbidity. As per the 1931 census, in India it was found that 72 per cent of marriages were performed before 15 years of age and 34 per cent before ten years of age. This resulted in a continuous increase in the mean age at marriage among males and females. The mean age of marriage of females has increased from 13.1 in 1901 to 18 years in 1991. Though, the mean age at marriage had been continuously increasing, yet a large number of girls even today marry at an age at which they are not ready for marriage either socially or emotionally.

Female literacy is highly correlated with proportion of population which is urban. Even districts with high female literacy tend to be more urbanized. In most of the districts of the major states in India, it was found that where a high proportion of women who could read and write the average number of children per woman were considerably lower than in districts where literacy levels were low. Also in high literacy districts, a greater proportion of children survived infancy. With every increase in the Indian population, the number of illiterate women also increases. In 1981, there were 181 million illiterate women in India and increases to 199 million in 1991. But, with every decade the percentage of literate women in India is also increasing from 9 per cent in 1951 to 39.5 per cent in 1991. Thus literacy is strongly correlated with the quality of life such as infant mortality rate, birth rate, death rate and the percentage of married females. Hence, it is fundamental to all-round development, material and spiritual.

Women Literacy and Development

To change women's situation, arousing the social consciousness is very important. In other words, improving the mother's status and make them socially aware, is vital to begin with the girls. Consciousness is related to understanding. The understanding of what is right and what is wrong. The understanding of what is rightfully one's own. When such understanding is attained, consciousness or awareness is generated. Thus social consciousness is the first step to fight injustice.

Nature has endowed all human beings with intelligence. Education and knowledge of the world make that intelligence sharper. Intelligence then becomes a power in women's hands. Many illiterate women are very intelligent, understanding and confident. However, things could have been different had they been educated.

It has been proved that literacy learning is not a technical exercise. It affects a whole range of attitudes and changes in perception and understanding of reality. The literate person tends to benefit more from different services. They are more open to put up new ideas into practice than their illiterate counterparts.

In today's society, life is to a large extent governed by money. To establish in such a society, women have to take up economic activities. Women should be self-reliant in economic matter which involves skills and expertise. Thus, education gives women a sense of their own identity. It opens the door to opportunity and choices and gives women the knowledge and skills to make the choices themselves.

Women have been accorded special treatment under the various rural development programmes to bring them into the main stream of development. One such effort is the Integrated Rural Development Programme (IRDP). The IRDP aims at improving the income position of the poor people in rural India by helping them to become self-employed in household enterprises, trades and professions. The training of rural youth for self-employment (TRYSEM) is a supporting component of IRDP. The TRYSEM enables people living below the poverty line to take up self-employment in different fields of activities. Under TRYSEM the minimum coverage of women has since been increased from 33 per cent to 40 per cent.

The programme of Development of Women and Children in Rural Areas (DWACRA) has its focus on rural women living below the poverty line. The DWACRA seeks to provide income generation activities to women by way of receiving system. A separate programme for women was considered necessary as it was noticed that women were not availing themselves of the IRDP benefits owing to various social constraints.

Conclusion

In spite of the above mentioned programmes, it is found that most of the government schemes sponsored by the Central Government particularly for the poor and women in rural areas cannot be implemented. The reason is that, most of the people are not aware of the government schemes. Ways and means to get the information is very limited. Though newspapers, radio and television play a major role in spreading information, but these cannot help them because they cannot read and write.

The root cause behind all these factors is because of their backwardness. Literacy thus has effective educational levels to total development of human values. To ensure women participation in the development process emphasis should be laid not only on literacy but also on empowering women through the awareness building programme. The only way out to overcome the growing imbalance between women and total development is through the acceleration of literacy.

REFERENCES

Asia-Pacific Population Policy, No. 15, dated December 1990.

Census of India, 1991, Paper-I Statement.

Handbook on Social Welfare Statistics, 1981.

"Literacy Population NEXUS", published by the Family Planning Association of India (Bombay, n.d.).

Literacy Mission, Vol. XV, No. 5, dated May 1992.

People and Planet, Vol. II, No. 1, 1993.

Population Education Newsletter, Quarterly, New Delhi, Vol. 7, Nos. 1 & 2, 1993.

SECTION II

Adult Education and Extension: Impact on Social Awareness

4

Awareness Generation Programme for Rural and Poor Women Held at Umroi, Mawngap and Laitdiengsai Villages:

East Khasi Hills District in Meghalaya

Introduction

Meghalaya attained its full-fledged State on the 21st January, 1972. The State comprises Khasi Hills, Jaintia Hills and the Garo Hills, lying between the longitudes 89.45°E and 92.47°E. The total area of the State is 22,429 sq.km. The total number of population according to the provisional census 2001 is 23,06,069.

The peoplc of Meghalaya belong to some of the earliest communities on the subcontinent, with their own traditions and customs. The Achiks (popularly known as Garos) and the Khasis and Jaintias are among the few communities in the world that observe the matrilineal line of descent in the family, in which lineage and ancestral property passes down from mother to daughter. The people of Meghalaya are both hardworking and fun-loving, fond of music as well as colourful ritual, respectful to tradition yet open to new ideas.

Before the advent of the British Rule, the Khasi and the Jaintia Hills districts were ruled by the *Syiems* and in Garo Hills by the *Laskars* and the *Nokmas*. Although, in Khasi Hills the institution of *Syiemship* still continues; and in Garo Hills that of the Laskarship and Nokmaship, but in Jaintia Hills district the *Dolois* ceased to persist after the Jaintia Hills territory was annexed by the British in 1835. In addition to the traditional institutions, there are other traditional village authorities known as *Lyngdoh, Sirdar* and *Wahadadar* who administered the *Elakas* (administrative areas) according to their respective customary laws and practice. Since all the traditional rulers in the Khasi and Jaintia Hills were elected by an electoral college; the people are politically conscious. This can be seen in the following pages.

Before we have a closer look on the awareness generation programme of the women in rural areas, let us look back on the role of women in the past in general.

The importance of women welfare services hardly needs emphasis. Late Pandit Jawaharlal Nehru remarked, "to awaken the people, it is the women who must be awakened. Once she is on the move, the family moves, the village moves and the nation moves".[1] Madan defines "women as the mother of the race and is the liaison between generations. Indian culture attaches much importance to this section of the society; therefore, India has been symbolised as mother India, keeping in view the exemplary qualities of women, namely patience, endurance, love, affection, sympathy and generosity."[2]

Pre-Independence Period

In ancient India, women were respected and held in high esteem. Their plight, however, became pitiable and their condition miserable with the passing of time. With the advent of British rule a new social era emerged. The Christian Missionaries brought a revolution in the society by highlighting the social evils existing with the Hindu social structure. While the Christian missionaries left their impact on the religious and social institutions, western education was responsible for the introduction of a new pattern of thinking whose major characteristics were rationalism, democracy and liberalism. During the British period there were two major movements which effected the position of women. These were the Social Reform Movement of the nineteenth century and the Nationalist Movement of the twentieth century. Both these movements raised the question of equal status of women. Raja

Rammohun Roy, the first social reformer, however, felt that these social evils should be eradicated by raising consciousness and making people sensitive to the injustice perpetrated on women. The other social reformers also championed the cause of women and the result was the certain social reforms undertaken by them to alleviate the suffering of women.[3]

Another very powerful force which helped changed the position and attitude towards women was the Nationalist Movement particularly during the Gandhian phase.[4] Certain Women Organizations also took up the cause of upliftment the status of women. The pre-independence period thus marked the beginning of awareness of the sufferings of women due to oppressive social customs. However, it is to be pointed out that the pace of women's welfare work during the British period was very slow and gained momentum only after independence.

After Independence

After independence all round efforts have been made to promote the welfare of women. Different classes of society were given special attention for the progress of women in India. Mahatma Gandhi and Pandit Jawaharlal Nehru had pleaded for equality, liberty and dignity of women. They were proud of the fact that large number of women especially from the villages had taken part in the freedom movement. But discrimination against women continued because of complex personal laws and customs, borrowed and inherited.[5]

The framers of the Constitution of India were well aware of the fact that the emancipation of women in India was a prerequisite for the socio-economic development of the country. This is enshrined in the preamble to the Constitution of India. Article 15 of the Constitution of India provides that, "the State shall not discriminate on the grounds of sex, caste etc., though the State could make any special provision for women." Under Article 16, women are equally eligible for all appointments under Article 39 of the Constitution relating to certain principles of policy to be followed by the State. Women have also equal rights to adequate means of livelihood and equal pay for equal work. Above all, the Constitution makes it a fundamental duty of every citizen, under Article 51A relating to fundamental duties to renounce practices derogatory to the dignity of women.[6] It is in the light of these provisions in the Constitution that social legislation had been passed to improve their status and rights.

Special steps had also been taken to improve their education, health facilities, economic position and for their proper participation in family and community life to bring women at par with men based upon our Constitution. Besides that, various laws were enacted to ensure equality, social justice and fraternity, enshrined in the preamble of the Constitution. Under the Constitution every citizen enjoys safeguard against exploitation and various measures have been taken up to ensure the protection and equal opportunity to women. But the noble ideals enshrined in the Constitution are hardly followed in practice. Women were not aware about the various programmes of social-welfare and development which is actually meant for their improvement. Policies to extent educational opportunities (both formal and non-formal) education to women have failed to bridge the knowledge gap between men and women which was emphasised as the main task by the National Committee on Women's Education in 1958.[7]

Further to train women for some gainful employment and to give them social education, certain women's programmes have been started after independence. The Community Development Programme (CDP) was launched in 1952, with an emphasis to improve women's participation in social life.[8] The programme were, however, judged successful and became the model for the extension of the programme throughout the country.

Major emphasis was also placed on different development projects for rural and urban areas for women. So, many programmes for women have been planned and also implemented such as 'Functional Literacy for Women', in 'Integrated Child Development Services Programme' under Ministry of Education and Culture, 'Condensed Courses for Women' launched by the Central Social Welfare Board, 'Special

Programme for Women' under Ministry of Education and Culture, etc. All these programmes were launched with the aims and objectives to educate women in making them more conscious of the rights and responsibilities. To fulfil these aims and objectives, sufficient preparation had been made such as human resources, planning and management, need based curriculum, sufficient teaching and learning materials, appropriate methodology, proper training, monitoring and evaluation etc.[9]

On the other hand, the Constitution of India gave women their equal rights with men from the beginning. Unfortunately, women in our country are mostly unaware of their rights because of illiteracy and the oppressive tradition. In order to create an awareness several efforts have been made to enhance the status of women from time to time. Women village workers and women social education organisers were appointed to promote social education and community participation in the department of Community Development. These workers were trained in Home Science to improve their skills, so that they might help the rural women with confidence. The Central Social Welfare Board started Welfare Extension Projects in 1954-55 to cover activities like social education, maternity and childcare, utilisation of leisure and recreational programmes. In 1971 the Committee on the status of women in India made a comprehensive review of the situation of women in India. The Committee, however, noted that dynamics of social change and development had adversely affected a large section, particularly the women. In accordance with this, the Ministry of Labour, Government of India, created a 'Women Cell' to prepare and co-ordinate policies and programmes on women employment and to implement the Equal Remuneration Act of the Government of India.[10]

From 1978-86, a number of working groups, task forces and national conferences were organised to discuss the issues of rural women, namely, Working Group on Development of Village. Level Organisation for Women (1978); Working Group for Employment of Rural Women (1978); National Conference on Women and Development (1979); committee to review and analyse the role and participation of Women in Eighties (1980);

Working Group on Personal Policies for bringing greater involvement of women in Science and Technology (1981); and Working Group on Women and Development (1983).[11] But in spite of all these efforts, women still lagged behind men in all fields.

According to 2001 Census, the total population of India showed at 866.87 million out of which 525.50 million (76.7%) lived in rural areas. Of the total population, females constituted (54.28%) and 253.72 million of these women belonged to rural areas, 77 per cent of the female population live in rural areas.

The "Awareness Generation Programme" was launched in three villages, viz., Umroi, Mawngap and Laitdiengsai in East Khasi Hills District of Meghalaya to know the level of awareness of the rural women in different aspects relating to their roles and functions.

As mentioned earlier, the Khasi, Jaintia and the Garo Society follows the matrilineal system. They reckon descent through the female line. Except in Meghalaya this system is not followed elsewhere in the North-Eastern Region of the country.

As such, the question of an illegitimate child is unknown in the Khasi society. The children take the name of their mother's clan, are members of her lineage and live in her social group. The matrilineal system signifies great reverence and respect to motherhood. True to the matrilineal principle, the Khasi, Jaintia and Garo Women occupy a honourable position in the society. A woman in Khasi society plays many important roles, her status is high. They could participate in all socio-cultural activities and events like dances, celebrations, funerals etc. The Khasi society shows its regard for women as important members of the socio-economic set-up. They have greater liberty to express themselves, they are accepted and treated as individuals. In the family more and more decision making power are equally shared by husband and wife.[12]

On the other hand, the Jaintia women like the Khasis occupies an honourable position in the society. The mother of a family looks after all the domestic affairs of the family. They do not only play a great role in domestic and religious affairs, but they actively participate in economic activities as well.[13] Unlike the Khasi and Jaintia Society the Garo Women's also followed the matrilineal system. In the field of administration women have no part at all which is similar to Khasi and Jaintia Community.[14]

When we take the overall picture of Khasi women we find that they are much better than their counterparts in any other patrilineal society. However, women are held in high esteem and regard; so, a mother holds a dignified position in the family. Incidentally, it may be recorded that a girl or her parents or both do not have much worry in the marriage preparation, as the dowry payment to the bridegroom does not exist in the society. In olden days all the property inherited from parents or acquired during the married couple's lifetime belongs to the woman. This does not connote that a Khasi woman considers herself superior to her husband and behaves aggressively. As a wife, she respects her husband and assist him in whatever way she can to make the family happy, after all, mutual love, trust, and respect are strong binding forces in married life.

On the other hand, in Khasi society women are not only treated more equally but in various social roles as mothers custodians of religion and property, they have an enviable place in society. Indeed, a Khasi woman does not assume to herself all the authorities in her family just because of what has been recorded above. In olden days, a husband was the lone bread-earner of the family. He supervised his wife's property, worked in the field and enjoyed his own privileges as a male member of the society. In his own clan, he may be a *Kni* or maternal uncle with a responsibility for the welfare of all the members of his clan. No marriage, no religious rites, no disposal of ancestral property could take place without his approval. In most cases, the *Kni* even today takes a decision in consultation with the other members of the family or clan according to the nature of his wisdom is required. Man, in whatever position: husbands or uncles are counsellor to their children, brothers, sisters, nephews and nieces. In fact, a good and responsible father was and is looked upon by his children as a bread-earner, a caretaker, a planner and in fact a maker of all good things for them.

Today society has seen a change in family relationship, attitude and values. One of the factors of change that has influenced the Khasi society is education. It is because of education women have spread out into various types of occupation. Shymali found out that the reason for taking up jobs was because of economic necessity rather than for any other reasons such as career or ambition or to achieve an independent status. However, she pointed out that women work because they feel the need to supplement their husband's income to make both ends meet.[15]

The accelerated social changes that overtook Khasi society is, by and large, mainly due to the progress of the Khasi women, their interest in education, economic independence, new aspiration for career in public life. With the modern modes of living and working more desires are coming up. Among the trading and cultivating Khasis, a husband now look after his wife and children. Among the educated and salaried classes, both husband and wife managed their families.

The study conducted by Saha and others showed that the Khasi women are enterprising and have taken up small-scale trades like fish, cloth and tea trades etc. Both in rural and urban areas, women are seen to be involved in wider economic activities. Educated women prefer for white-collar jobs. The Khasi women are out in the new situation to have economic independence. They do not like to be burdens upon their husbands.[16]

Keeping all these considerations in view, the 'Awareness Generation Programme' was conducted at Umroi (*Mylliem Syiemship*), Laitdiengsai (*Khyrim Syiemship*) and Mawngap (*Marbisu Sardarship*) of the East Khasi Hills district of Meghalaya.

The main objectives of the awareness generation camps for the rural and poor women were to orient them to the development programmes; to equip them with the knowledge, attitudes and skills necessary for implementing the Generation Awareness Programme; to motivate and prepare them for further preparation. Learning and planning for the programmes relevant to their own areas; and to introduce them to relevant resources based on their own region with a view to creating a cadre of socially conscious women from among the poor.

Methodology

Before holding each camp, initial survey was conducted by visiting a few villages which could be grouped together. Thus, for the Umroi camp nearby villages, namely Umden, Umeit, Umsawriang, Nongrah and Mawthei were also the beneficiaries as trainees were drawn from each village. For the Mawngap camp localities like Mawngaprim, Mawngap Dukan, Mawngap Mawsmai, Mawkharshiing and Mawmyrsiang were the beneficiaries. Similarly, for the Laitdiengsai camp too nearby villages of Rableng, Laitkyrhong, Rangphlang, Rasong and Laityam sent trainees.

During the survey as well as in the launching of the programme leaders of various social organisations and headmen were directly involved. Discussions with presidents and secretaries of welfare organisations, especially of women, were helpful as information about various social problems in the rural areas was made known to the organisers of the camp. Names of trainees, too, were recommended by those leaders. They were very keen that those trainees should serve as catalysts in their respective villages and localities after the training camps.

Thirty women participated in each camp. These were within the age group of 25-42. The group was heterogeneous by nature; and all in the group were able to read and write Khasi legibly. The discussions held with the women after each lecture afforded the organisers with valuable data about the problems experienced by the women in the society. In brief, the problems are health, socio-economic and political.

The course content of the workshops was designed according to the guidelines chalked out by the Central Social Welfare Board, Government of India. The workshop lasted for five days in each of the three camps. The programme was co-ordinated with the CACE., North-Eastern Hill University,

Shillong, certain key development departments of the Government of Meghalaya and the State Bank of India. Experts in various disciplines relevant with the programme were invited to deliver lectures to the trainees in all the three camps.

Apart from the lectures and the discussion following it, the organisers distributed questionnaire of 18 questions pertaining to the programme to all the trainees. The tables appended to the present study give the feedback from the trainees.

Programme

The course in each camp contained the following topics: (i) Status of Women; (ii) Women and the Law; (iii) Women and Health; (iv) Community Health and Hygiene; (v) Women, Technology and Environment; (vi) Women and Economy; (vii) Women and the State Government; (viii) Women, Religion and Culture; (ix) Women and Social Action, and (x) Women and Education.

Table 4.1: Showing Marital Status

Category	*Status*	*Percentage*
1. Married with children	72	80.00
2. Married but with no child	6	6.67
3. Having only one child	12	13.33
Number of Trainees	90	100.00

Table 4.2: Showing Profession

Category	*Status*	*Percentage*
1. Office work	7	7.78
2. Agriculture	65	72.22
3. Trade and shop-keeping	5	5.56
4. Tailoring	2	2.22
5. Poultry and Piggery	1	1.11
6. Daily wage	1	1.11
7. No profession	9	10.00
Number of trainees	90	100.00

Table 4.3: Showing the Benefits from the Training

Category	*Status*	*Percentage*
1. Much benefited	67	74.44
2. Just for a lesson	1	1.11
3. Please to meet friends	1	1.11
4. Blank	3	3.34
5. Marked more than one box	18	20.00
Number of Trainees	90	100.00

Analysis of the Data

Out of the nine tables in the preceding chapter, four of them deserve a close analysis to enable policy makers and economic planners to realise the magnitude of the social problems faced by women in particular and the society in general.

The response of the trainees to question relating to the need to boil water as per Table 4.4, before drinking is encouraging if we consider only those ninety women who participated in the training programme. The possibility of a large number of people who never boil water is there in the remote and inaccessible areas of the East Khasi Hills District. Those ninety women are expected to carry the message they got to their respective village because 81 of the 90 knew that boiled water is disease free.

Table 4.4: Showing Habit in Drinking Water

Category	*Status*	*Percentage*
1. Always boil water	73	81.11
2. Sometimes	5	5.56
3. Never boil water	10	11.11
4. No response	2	2.22
Number of Trainees	90	100.00

Table 4.5: Showing Domestic Cooking Arrangement

Category	*Status*	*Percentage*
1. Fireplace with firewood	67	74.44
2. Sawdust	3	3.33
3. Kerosene oil	2	2.23
4. Charcoal and chawla	3	3.33
5. Firewood and Chimney	7	7.78
6. No response	8	8.89
Number of Trainees	90	100.00

Table 4.6: Showing Sanitary Awareness/Kinds of Latrines Used

Category	*Status*	*Percentage*
1. Septic tank	9	10.00
2. Pit	23	25.56
3. Nothing	48	53.33
4. No Response	10	11.11
Number of Trainees	90	100.00

As per Table 4.6, it is discouraging to note that as many as 53.33 per cent of the participants do not even use pit latrines in their villages. Even the 11.11 per cent who did not respond might not have made any arrangement for latrine and they avoided to respond most probably out of shame.

Table 4.7: Showing Beneficiaries from Bank Loan

Category	*Status*	*Percentage*
1. Beneficiaries	36	40.00
2. Non-beneficiaries	52	57.77
3. No response	2	2.23
Number of Trainees	90	100.00

Table 4.7 shows that in so far as loan from banks is concerned it depends on the need and the capacity of the people to utilize the loan money judiciously and the will to repay it. The fact that as much as 40 per cent of the ninety women got loan from banks show that most of the people are aware of the

facilities offered by banks, especially after bank nationalisation in 1969.

Table 4.8: Showing Need for Sending Children to School

Category	*Status*	*Percentage*
1. Yes	85	94.44
2. No response	5	5.56
Number of Trainees	90	100.00

Table 4.9: Showing Problems in Educating Children

Category	*Status*	*Percentage*
1. No Problem	5	5.56
2. Poverty	70	77.78
3. Too young	3	3.33
4. Cost of Living	1	1.11
5. No school/college in the village	5	5.56
6. No response	6	6.66
Number of Trainees	90	100.00

The main problem for parents to send their children to school because of poverty is highlighted in Table 4.9. As much as 77.78 per cent indicated the fact, and only 5.56 per cent were able to bear the cost of education. Primary education, except in private schools, is free in Meghalaya. The cost of books is not that high yet; moreover, primary education is imparted in the morning only, usually 7.00 a.m. to 11.00 a.m. Poor parents could not afford to spare their children even during that period because they are made to look after their younger brothers and sisters as their parents are busy in their profession. Grown up children have to assist their parents in other domestic works like cooking, washing clothes and utensils, fetching water also.

Those few who sent their children to schools found it difficult to send them for further education. If a village has only primary school, then for middle and high school education they have to send them elsewhere meaning having two establishments. The opening of a high school or a college in any village depends also on the availability of feeder schools, otherwise the preparedness to encourage their children for further study at home seems reasonable. When examined further the root cause is the same: poverty, or that the families does not have enough to spare for the higher education of their children.

The trained women were fully aware of the major problems faced by the Khasi society. Twenty-one of them underlined drunkenness and gambling as the worst enemies of the society; 15 underlined poverty. There was a feeling that villages must have public latrines financed by the Government. Granted that there may be government, state or local-self, which would venture to do it, the question of maintenance of such latrines in rural areas will remain to be realized only when one is constructed. The absence of a jeepable or good roads connecting a few villages was mentioned by a few women. Indeed, in time when a patient needs to be rushed to dispensaries or hospitals for treatment, the absence of the road and means of transport can cost a life.

Two of the women expressed concern over the lack of opportunity to have any part in the traditional village durbars. This kind of durbar is different from public meetings where women also participated. According to tradition, only men who attained the age of maturity called upon to participate in a village *durbar*. If a change takes place, most women can express themselves against social evils associated mostly with men.

Except seven, all the other women sincerely longed to improve upon their socio-economic life. The responses to possible steps to be taken vary according to the interests and knowledge of the respondents. That tailoring and weaving must be encouraged by the state was suggested by 27 women; ten others believed that potato processing machines will help to improve the lot of the people since potato is one of the major crops in Khasi Hills. Eight were in favour of poultry, piggery and agriculture to be encouraged by the government. Only three strongly felt the need to have a night school and a night college in their village. Most of the respondents had the state Government in mind.

One interesting question on which most of the ninety women had expressed themselves clearly is wanton destruction of forests in the Khasi Hills District. Their suggestions deserve attention. Thirty-six of them were in favour of allowing trees to grow in the forest. As the suggestions were written by themselves the translation from the Khasi language is "don't cut trees at all". The sentence is hypothetical: it could mean that it is, and it could also mean that young trees should not be destroyed. Indeed eight other women suggested the second alternative, and six other urged that forest should not be destroyed mercilessly. The process of replacement of mature trees was mooted out by 12 who insisted the old one must be used and new ones must be planted; 12 others suggested that one tree must be planted in areas where no trees are available. Seventeen women wrote to explain that destruction of forest deprives people of water and natural manure.

Their suggestions remain only as suggestions because the majority of the trainees used firewood for cooking purposes. Until such time that electric power or gas is made to replace firewood, the problem continues.

"What could be the duties of a mother to the society at large?" This question attracted several items of what women in rural areas could do; and each women suggested more than three items of job. We simply list the suggestions to see what the trainees had in mind when they responded to our question: (1) to keep the house clean; (2) to participate in social works; (3) to discuss with others all the issues of general interests; (4) women should have no organisation; (5) women must be allowed to take part in village durbar; (6) to teach others the value of social co-operation; (7) to be watchful of what happen in the village; (8) to help in a drive to prohibit the consumption of alcohol; (9) to help the family and the society; and (10) women must know how to conduct themselves.

Needless to say, in spite of their major contribution in society, women fall victims to the predicament of their unequal status. It is women, among the unequals in society, who are victimised and discriminated to the maximum on each step. Men, whether dominant or subordinate have always tried to keep women in their perpetual subordination and innumerable oppressive measures. Consequently, women, on the one hand, are exploited by men who claim to be superior. On the other hand, her potentialities are not fully realised due to the constraints as evolved and institutionalised by men. Women, however, constitute one of the most important and dynamic but deprived and long neglected section of the society. Under pressure and forces of traditional cultural and historical factors, women have been ignored and denied opportunities participating in the process of development and sharing its benefits. The women's place is still considered to be in the home not in school or at jobs.

If we analyse the reasons behind it for what women are suffering a lot in our society, the main answer would be ignorance, lack of education is the main cause for which women are the sufferer than men. Social factors also plays an important role in inhabiting the participation of women in education. Most important, however, is the attitude towards girl which is widely prevalent, especially among the poor and in rural areas. The role of girls is restricted and considered to be useful both by the parents and the community. Hence, there is low participation of girls in education. On the other hand, as boys are regarded as belonging to the world of work, their education is encouraged. Again women are regarded to be passive in social system which confers on them a subordinate status and their education is feared as it may make the woman question such a system, hence the negative attitude towards women's education. The equal rights and protection for both men and women already mentioned in our Constitution are not applicable in practical life.

Suggestions

More funds are required to organise more training camps in their villages every year. A follow-up programme also is necessary and this too need fund.

The State government, the District Council and the traditional heads like the *syiem* and his *durbar* have a great deal to do to check the social evils mentioned by the women.

Public representatives and members of the society who have some education will do well to educate the women folks of the facilities extended by financing institutions, and responsibility it entails.

Village *durbars* may have to take some positive steps to educate people of the danger of making open spaces as latrines.

In some big village, evening schools and non-formal education at the elementary levels would help to remove illiteracy. This need the attention of the village *durbars* and the State government.

Since most trainees wanted to improve their socio-economic life, leaders of public opinion and officers of development departments would do well to give wide publicity or the various assistances, technical and financial, extended by the government every year.

Health education to be given priority in the rural areas. Full participation of women in their respective local *Durbar Shnong* (Village Durbar) is needed.

NOTES

1. Vidyulata, *Developing Rural Women (A Case Study of Trysem)*, Discovery Publishing House, New Delh, 1990, p. 1.
2. Madan, G.R., *Indian Social Problems—Social Disorganisation and Reconstruction*, Vol. II, Allied Publishers Pvt. Ltd., Calcutta, 1967, p. 112.
3. Desai, Neera *et al.*, *Women and Society in India*, Ajanta Publication Delhi, 1987, p. 39.
4. *Ibid.*
5. *Arunachal Newsletter* (*Naharlagun*), Vol. V, No. 72 dated 27 March, 1989, p. 3.
6. Allahabad Law Agency, *Constitution of India as Amended Up-To-Date*, Allahabad Law Agency, Allahabad, 1987, pp. 4-5.
7. Bhowmik, K.L. (Edn.), *Development of Women and Children*, Inter-India Publications, New Delhi, 1988, p. 101.
8. Mehra, Rekha *et al.*, *Women and Rural Transformation—Two Studies*, Concept Publishing Company, New Delhi, 1983, pp. 4-7.
9. Bhowmik, K.L. (ed.), *op. cit.*, pp. 101-102.
10. Vidyulata, *Developing Rural Women*, Discovery Publishing House, New Delhi, 1990, pp. 5-6.
11. *Ibid.*, pp. 6-7.

12. War, J., "Status of Women in Traditional Khasi Culture", a Seminar paper on Status of Women in Tribal Cultures of Meghalaya on 13-14 July, 1988, organised by the Centre for Literary and Cultural Studies, NEHU in collaboration with Indian Council of Social Science Research, NERC, Shillong.
13. Passah, P.M., "Status of Women in the Jaintia Culture", *Ibid.*, pp. 1-2.
14. Marak, C.R. "Status of Women in the Garo Cultures", *Ibid.*, pp. 4-6.
15. Datta, Shymali, *Khasi Working Women of Shillong*, M.Phil dissertation, 1985 (unpublished).
16. Mukherjee, B. *et al.*, "The Tribal Amazons in Matrilineal Society" in the *Tribal Women in India*, Indian Anthropological Society, Calcutta, 1978, p. 178.

5

Impact of Adult Education Programmes in Promoting Social Awareness

Introduction

Adult Education (Liveright and Maygood, 1968:9) is conceived as a process thereby the uneducated adults are imparted with skills of identifying and solving their personal and community problems. National Adult Education Programme (NAEP) consisted of three basic components, viz., literacy, functionality and awareness. Literacy aimed at promoting skills of reading, writing and simple arithmetic among the learners. Functionality is concerned with development of knowledge and skills related to production of activities of the learners. Social awareness means to spread the knowledge of the learners on issues related to social, political and economic problems.

About 230 million of adult population are illiterate. These form mostly the poorest and the most neglected sections of the nations. Their condition is such that they are not able to take advantage of the benefits available to them under the development plans. These illiterate adults continue to be exposed to exploitation and social disabilities. Without making them aware of the problems faced by them and their communities it is not possible to motivate them for acquiring literacy skills and participating in adult education programme. Awareness is the most significant element in the NAEP and the adult education functionaries and others require to have a clear perception of the meaning and scope of awareness.

Adult Education programme is the community-oriented programme. Now the question arises. Why is it necessary to educate the adults? The reason is because illiteracy retards the growth and development of a country. Illiteracy affects the country in three ways, viz., economically, politically and socially. Economically, an educated farmer is capable of raising his agricultural production to a greater extent than an uneducated farmer. Politically, India is a democratic country where the masses play a vital role in the government. If the voter is illiterate, he does not know whom he votes and why? Socially, illiterate people are depressing because of health condition. Communicable diseases like malaria, small-pox and cholera take a heavy toll of life and people in general. It is only through proper education that can dispel this ignorance and superstition and help them to raise the standards of living.

Mention may be made that three-fourth of the Indian population live in rural areas but their living conditions are far from satisfactory. Poverty, ignorance, superstitions, illiteracy, and ill health are found to be on mass scale. Primarily, rural community lives on agriculture. The scheme of adult education, which tries to teach them the three Rs, is not at all useful. They do not find any gain in learning simple alphabets and numbers. They are in need of such literacy programme which will cater their needs and help them to develop their productivity and also help them for their livelihood.

Since the real problem of adult education exists in the rural areas, an attempt is made to find out how effective the adult education programme being implemented have an impact in the areas of social awareness. The analysis on social awareness is based on the responses of the community people on four major issues, viz., adult education programme and its related issues, health issues, community participation and awareness on social life. Hence, it was decided to carry out the study on impact of Adult Education programme in promoting social awareness.

Universe

The special concern of the present study is the four villages chosen from two blocks of the East Khasi Hills District in Meghalaya as the locale for study. The blocks selected are:

(1) Mawkynrew Block and (2) Khadarshnong Laitkroh Block. From each block, two villages have been selected on random basis from the list of the Block Development Officers supplied by the Community and Rural Development Department, Government of Meghalaya, Shillong. From Mawkynrew Block, the villages selected are: (1) Thangsning Village and (2) Jongksha Village. From Khadarshnong Laitkroh Block, the villages selected are: (1) Kyrdem Khla Village, and (2) Laitkynsew Village. These are the villages where the literacy programme or various awareness generating programmes have been launched either by the educational institutions, the State Government or by the Non-Governmental organization for people's development.

Materials and Methods

Primary data was used for the analysis of the study. The study decided to collect a sample of 140 respondents from the four villages under two blocks. Investigation of a total sample of seventy from each block was carried out through face-to-face contact with the respondents. The tools used for the collection of primary data were interview schedule in the form of a structure questionnaires and observational (non-participants). The 140 sample respondents have been selected on the basis of "Simple Random Sampling Technique", and are discussed together. The secondary data for the study have been collected from articles, books, journals and other available relevant materials. Data collected from the selected respondents of the two blocks of the East Khasi Hills District are interpreted and analysed here as under:

1. Socio-Economic Background of the Respondents

Of a total 140 (100%) respondents, 50.72 per cent are males and 49.28 per cent were females. As regards age group 55.72 per cent are in the age group of 30 years above. Another 29.28 per cent under the age of 15-30 years and 15 per cent under the age group of below 15 years.

Regarding literacy, of a total 140 (100%) 55 per cent are illiterate, 37.86 per cent are below matriculate and only 7.14 per cent are matriculate, pre-university and very few are graduate.

As regards marital status, 75 per cent are married and 24.29 per cent are not yet married. Out of 75 per cent married respondents, only 0.71 per cent are divorce. As regards religion 47.85 per cent belong to the indigenous religion. While a majority of 52.15 per cent are predominantly Christians. No other religion like Hindus, Muslims, etc. of other faith are found prevalent in these villages under study. As regards occupation, only 8.56 per cent are doing business; 2.14 per cent are government employees and 2.84 per cent are professional services. A large majority of 47.14 per cent are working as farmers; 20.71 per cent worked as daily wage labourers and 18.56 per cent are non-earners. As regards monthly income 56.15 per cent earned below Rs. 500 per month; 25.43 per cent earned between Rs. 500 to Rs. 1000 per month; while 9.64 per cent earned between Rs. 1000 to 2000 per month. Only 8.78 per cent earned more than Rs. 2000 per month. Thus, the data collected reveals that majority of the people in the rural areas are poor.

2. *Impact of Social Awareness*

The data (Table 5.1) reveals that out of 140 (100%) only 29.28 per cent are aware about the adult education programme, while a large majority of 70.72 per cent are not aware at all what adult education programme is all about. Of these 29.28 per cent who are aware about the adult education programme a further query was made.

Table 5.1: Awareness of the Respondents on the Query "Have you heard about the Adult Education Programme"?

Responses	*Mawkynrew Block*	*Laitkroh Block*	*Total*	*Percentage*
Yes	31	10	41	29.28
No	39	60	99	70.72
Total	**70**	**70**	**140**	**100.00**

The data on Table 5.2 reveals that out of 41 (29.28%), only 24.31 per cent are aware about the National Adult Education Programme, while a majority of 75.61 per cent are not aware at all. This shows that awareness of the respondents is poor. With regards to literacy programme, the data reveals that 53.65 per cent are aware about literacy programme, while 46.35 per cent are not aware at all. This shows that the awareness

Table 5.2: Awareness of the Respondents on the Query "Discussion in your Community Centre on Adult Education"?

Responses		*Maw-kynrew Block*	*Lait-kroh Block*	*Total*	*Per-centage*
National Adult Education	Yes	10	0	10	24.39
Programme	No	21	10	31	75.61
Literacy	Yes	21	1	22	53.65
	No	10	9	19	46.35
Post Literacy	Yes	11	0	11	26.82
	No	20	10	30	73.18
Continuing Education	Yes	14	0	14	34.14
	No	17	10	27	65.86
Population Education	Yes	11	0	11	26.82
	No	20	10	30	73.18
Fertilizers and Chemicals	Yes	16	0	16	39.02
	No	15	10	25	60.98
Improved Quality of Seeds	Yes	20	0	20	48.78
	No	11	10	21	51.22
Farm Equipments	Yes	12	0	12	29.26
	No	19	10	29	70.74
Artificial Insemination	Yes	8	0	8	19.51
	No	23	10	33	80.49
Total		**31**	**10**	**41**	**100.00**

on literacy is average. Regarding post-literacy, the data collected indicates that only 26.82 per cent are aware about post literacy programme, while a majority of 73.18 per cent are not aware at all. Thus the data shows that awareness is very low. As regard continuing education, the data shows that only 34.14 per cent are aware about continuing education, while a majority of 65.86 per cent are not aware at all. The data thus indicates that awareness is poor. With regard to population education, the data reveals that only 26.82 per cent are aware about population education, while a majority of 65.86 per cent are not aware about population education. This shows that awareness is very poor. With regard to fertilizers and chemicals, the data shows that 39.02 per cent are aware about the use of fertilizers and chemicals in agriculture, while 60.98 per cent are not aware at all. This indicates that awareness is very low. As regard improved quality of seeds, the data reveals that 48.78 per cent are aware how to improve their own skills while 51.22 per cent are not aware at all. This indicates that awareness is not satisfactory. As regard farm equipment, the data shows that only 29.26 per cent are aware about the use of equipments, while a majority of 70.74 per cent have no knowledge about equipments.

This shows that awareness is poor. Regarding artificial insemination, the data collected reveals that only 19.51 per cent are aware about insemination, while a majority of 80.49 per cent are not aware at all. This shows that awareness is very poor. Thus, the study reveals that the over all impact of the awareness programme on adult education is not satisfactory.

Data on Table 5.3 below reveals that out of 41 (29.28%), 48.78 per cent are aware that adult education programme has helped them to increase their functionality, while 51.22 per cent are not aware what is functionality, not to speak of the increase of functionality in their day-to-day life, which shows that awareness on functionality is very low.

Table 5.3: Awareness of the Respondents on the Query "Has the National Adult Education Programme helped you in anyway to Increase your Level of Functionality"?

Responses	*Mawkynrew Block*	*Laitkroh Block*	*Total*	*Percentage*
Yes	20	0	20	48.78
No	11	10	21	51.22
Total	**31**	**10**	**41**	**100.00**

Table 5.4 will measure the level of awareness to which the respondents have acquired knowledge about adult education programme. Out of 41 (29.28%) only 39.02 per cent

of the data collected indicates that programmes on adult education have helped them to eradicate illiteracy, while 60.98 per cent are not aware at all. This shows that awareness is very low. As regards raising their income, the data reveals that 31.71 per cent are aware about this, while a majority of 68.29 per cent are not aware that literacy level helps to increase the level of income. This shows that awareness is poor. Further, 26.82 per cent mentioned that adult education programme helped them to get better job opportunities, while a large majority of 73.18 per cent indicates of not aware at all. Thus, the data reveals that awareness is very poor. As regards raising their social status, the data indicates that only 36.58 per cent are aware about this, while majority of 63.42 per cent are not aware that functional literacy helps them to raise their social status. This shows that awareness is not satisfactory. Regarding increasing their knowledge on population related issues, the data collected indicates that 38.02 per cent are aware about population related issues, while 60.98 per cent shows that they have no knowledge on population related issues. This shows that the over all awareness on functional literacy is not an encouraging one. This impact of social awareness programmes is evident in the knowledge increase of the people on the adult education related issues.

Table 5.4: Awareness of the Respondents on the Query "Has the Adult Education Programme helped you in Eradication of"?

Responses		*Maw-kynrew Block*	*Lait-kroh Block*	*Total*	*Per-centage*
Illiteracy	Yes	16	0	16	39.02
	No	15	10	25	60.98
In raising your income	Yes	13	0	13	31.71
	No	18	10	28	68.29
Better job opportunities	Yes	11	0	11	26.82
	No	20	10	30	73.18
Raising your Social Status	Yes	15	0	15	36.58
	No	16	10	26	68.42
Increasing your Knowledge	Yes	16	0	16	39.02
on Population Related Issues	No	15	10	25	60.98
Total		**31**	**10**	**41**	**100.00**

Impact of Social Awareness on Health

Adult education programmes have been unsuccessful in the past because adult literacy is not placed within a wider social context. The whole gamut of the developmental needs of the adult of survival employment, health, etc. are not addressed. There is failure to realize that illiteracy is but a form of marginalization or exclusion of those who are unable to secure for themselves minimum standards of well-being. The problem has been viewed more in the context of teaching methods and of learning to read and write. Table 5.5 indicates the social awareness of the respondents on health.

Table 5.5: Awareness of the Respondents on the Query "Is there any Public Health Centre in your Locality"?

Responses	*Mawkynrew Block*	*Laitkroh Block*	*Total*	*Percentage*
Yes	62	6	68	48.57
No	8	64	72	51.43
Total	**70**	**70**	**140**	**100.00**

The data (Table 5.5) collected in this regard shows that out of a total 140 (100%) respondent, 48.57 per cent are aware that public health centre (PHC) is available in the locality, while 51.43 per cent are not aware about the PHC in their locality. Thus, the data collected shows that awareness of the respondents about community health centre is very low.

Table 5.6 indicates that out of 68 (48.57%), the data collected indicates that 75 per cent of the respondents are aware about the availability of medicine in the PHC, while 25 per cent shows that no medicine is available in the PHC. This shows that awareness on medicine is very good. Further, the data shows that only 2.95 per cent of the respondents are aware that laboratory test is available in the PHC, while a large majority of 97.05 per cent stated that no facilities of laboratory test is available in the PHC. On enquiry during investigation it was found that no medical test facility is available in the PHC. Thus the data collected reveals that the awareness of the respondents on laboratory test is very good. The data further reveals that only 26.47 per cent are aware the availability of beds in the PHC, while a majority of 73.53 per cent mentioned that no bed was available in the PHC. On inquiry during investigation it was found that there was no provision of beds in the hospitals for the community patient. This shows that the awareness of the respondents is good. As regards the distribution of birth control devices, the data reveals that 13.24 per cent are aware about the birth control methods, while 86.7 per cent are not aware about the distribution of birth control devices. Thus, the data collected indicates that awareness of the respondents is very low. Regarding doctors' attendance the data indicates that 36.76 per cent are aware about the attendance of doctors in the PHC, while 63.24 per cent are not aware at all. This shows that awareness of the respondents is not satisfactory. With regard to medical attendants, the data reveals that 97.06 per cent of the health workers are available in the PHC, while only 2.94 per cent are not aware about the availability of the medical attendants in the health centre. Thus, the data collected reveals that awareness of the respondents

Table 5.6: Awareness of the Respondents on the Query "If Yes, Facilities Available in Your Health Centre"?

Responses		*Maw-kynrew Block*	*Lait-kroh Block*	*Total*	*Per-centage*
Medicine	Yes	45	6	51	75.00
	No	17	17	17	25.00
Laboratory Test	Yes	2	0	2	2.95
	No	60	6	66	97.05
Availability of Beds	Yes	12	6	18	26.47
	No	50	0	50	73.53
Distribution of Birth	Yes	7	2	9	13.24
Control Device	No	55	4	59	86.76
Doctor	Yes	19	6	25	36.76
	No	43	0	43	63.24
Medical Attendants	Yes	60	6	66	97.06
	No	2	0	2	2.94
Nurses	Yes	25	6	31	45.58
	No	37	0	37	54.42
Total		**62**	**6**	**68**	**100.00**

on medical attendants is very good. With regard to nurses facility in the PHC the data indicates that 45.53 per cent are aware about nurses facility, while another 54.42 per cent indicates of not aware about nurses facility in the PHC. Thus, the data shows that awareness of the respondents about nurses facility is average. From the data collected, the study indicates that the overall impact of awareness programme on health is satisfactory.

Table 5.7 below indicates that out of 68 (48.57%) majority of the respondents are aware that no meal is served to the patient in the PHC. Thus, the data given below indicates that awareness of respondents on the provision of food in the PHC is very good.

Table 5.7: Awareness of the Respondents on the Query "Are Meals Served"?

Responses	*Mawkynrew Block*	*Laitkroh Block*	*Total*	*Percentage*
Yes	0	0	0	0.00
No	62	6	68	100.00
Total	**62**	**6**	**68**	**100.00**

In order to understand better the condition of other respondents who mentioned that no PHC is available in the locality, a query was further made to find out how these respondents procure their medical facilities.

The data on Table 5.8 below indicates that out of 72 (51.43%) of the respondents, only 13.88 per cent indicates of procuring their medicines from the local medical doctor while 86.12 per cent mentioned of not aware about the local medical doctor. Thus, the data indicates that awareness of the respondents on local medical doctor is poor.

Further, the data collected indicates that 95.83 per cent of the respondents procure their medical facilities from the nearby village, while only 4.17 per cent indicates of not aware about the availability of doctors in the nearby village. This shows that awareness of the respondents is good. While interacting with the community people face to face they informed that local doctors are not regular in coming to the locality. Most of the time they have to go to the nearby village for medical check-up and to procuring medicines during illness from the private doctors. Moreover, these respondents informed that many a times during emergency they have to go to the district headquarters for medicines. Thus, the data reveals the fact that 93.05 per cent of the respondents procure medicines from the district headquarters while 6.95 per cent indicates their inability to go to the district headquarters for medicine because of poverty. Further, the data reveals that 3.57 per cent of the respondents have to travel for medical treatment to 2 kms; 13.57 per cent travel for 2 to 5 kms. and 82.86 per cent informed they have to travel more than 5 kms. for medicines and for medical check-up. The data collected thus, indicates that medical facilities available in the village are very poor.

Table 5.8: Awareness of the Respondents on the Query "If No, from Where you Procure Your Medical Facilities"?

Responses		*Maw-kynrew Block*	*Lait-kroh Block*	*Total*	*Per-centage*
Local Medical Doctor	Yes	5	5	10	13.88
	No	3	59	62	86.12
From nearby Village	Yes	8	61	69	95.83
	No	0	3	3	4.17
At District Headquarters	Yes	8	59	67	93.05
	No	0	5	5	6.95
I have to go for Medical	2 Kms. or less	3	2	5	3.57
Treatment to	2 to 5 Kms.	10	9	19	13.57
	No	37	0	37	54.42
	More than 5 Kms.	57	59	116	82.86
	Total	**8**	**64**	**72**	**100.00**

Concluding Remarks

The study reveals that out of 100 per cent of the respondents, 55 per cent are illiterate. Among the literate very few have reached eight or ten standards. A majority of them studies up to class III or IV standards. Among the matriculate, only

2.85 per cent are graduates and are working as School Teachers in the village. Further, the data reveals that 47.14 per cent are working as farmers while 20.71 per cent worked as daily wage labourers. A majority of 56.15 per cent earned below Rs.500 per month. The Planning Commission of India states "Families of five members with an average annual income of Rs. 6,400 and below are classified as poverty families". Thus, the study reveals that 56.15 per cent of the people live below the poverty line.

Social awareness as the second major component of adult education aims at enlightening the learner about the existing reality to overcome the problems. Adult education helps the learners to play an active role in their own development. The study of awareness on adult education shows that out of 100 per cent a majority of the respondents 70.61 per cent are not aware about adult education of those who are aware, only 53.65 per cent are aware literacy programme; 26.82 per cent are aware post literacy; 34.14 per cent are aware about continuing education; 26.82 per cent are aware about population education; 39.02 per cent are aware about the use of fertilizers and chemicals; 48.78 per cent are aware of the improvement on the quality of seeds, 29.26 per cent are aware about farm equipments and only 19.51 per cent are aware about artificial insemination. Thus, the study shows that the overall impact of social awareness on adult education programme is very negligible. In spite of the stress made on promoting social awareness, it was identified by the earlier studies that enough emphasis was not given in practice in promoting social awareness among the learners. Silvadasan Pillai's study (1990: 134-135) pointed out that only 21 per cent of the learners were able to experience a change in their social attitude.

The performance of the local community concerned with functionality is very poor. The study reveals that only 48.78 per cent are aware about functionality. Those who are aware about functionality, the study shows that 39.02 per cent has helped them to eradicate illiteracy; 31.71 per cent has been able to raise their income; 26.82 per cent has helped them to raise their social status and 39.02 pert cent enable them to increase the knowledge about population related issues. This shows that the overall awareness on the impact of functionality is very discouraging.

Ever since the introduction of NAEP, functionality has been recognized as one of the three major components of adult education. Despite the importance given to functionality, the areas of functionality to be covered by adult education are not specified by policy documents. The studies of Tiwari (1978) and Vasudeva rao (1984) pointed out that functionality did not receive enough importance in the implementation of adult education. Very few studies touched upon the impact of adult education on functionality levels of the learners. Lack of specific guidelines on areas of functionality to be imparted in adult education would be the reason for this. Rao *et al*. (1980) confirmed that only literacy received attention in adult education while functionality was most neglected. According to Natarajan (1982), the programme failed to stress on the development of functional knowledge and skills among the learners.

The awareness on areas of health care among the local community is not good. Out of 140 (100%) respondents 48.57 per cent are aware that PHC is available in their locality. Of those as many as 75 per cent indicates that medicines are available in the PHC. A large majority of 97.05 per cent are aware that there is no laboratory test in the primary health centre. A big percentage of 73.53 per cent are aware that there is no bed facility in the PHC. Only a small percentage of 13.24 per cent are aware the distribution of birth control devices. Another 36.76 per cent are aware the attendance of doctors in the PHC. A large percentage of 97.06 per cent are aware that there is a medical attendant in the PHC. Then, 45.58 per cent are aware about nurses in the PHC. Molly Mathew and Sree Kumar (1990:504) in their analysis of the study of social awareness in terms of awareness of the learners in areas of health and family planning conducted that 51 per cent of the learners had no knowledge of proper health habits and only 12 per cent of the learners were aware of some methods of family planning. The study of Molley Mathew *et al.* is proved to be true even in the case of the village study in Meghalaya. The area under study shows that 51.43 per cent of the respondents are not aware of PHC. Those who are aware

(48.57%) of PHC, only 13.24 per cent have knowledge of the distribution of birth control devices.

In identification of the social problems like health care to those respondents who are not aware of PHC in their locality, the data reveals that only 13.88 per cent are aware about the local medical doctor. A vast majority of 95.83 per cent procured their medicines from the nearby village and 93.05 per cent from the district headquarters. Respondents who procure medicines from the nearby village and from the district headquarters, 3.57 per cent stated they have to travel for 2 kms. for medical treatment; 13.57 per cent travel 5 kms. and 82.86 per cent travel more than 5 kms. Meghalaya with population of 1.8 million is predominantly rural (81.41%). Little has been achieved with half the population continue to live below the poverty line. Though, there has been a steady decline in the death rate, improvement in life expectancy and an increase in health infrastructure, but 42.3 per cent of the State's population is still uncovered by health care. Though, there are 85 primary health centres (PHCs) and 324 health sub-centres (SCs) in Meghalaya but as many as 60-70 per cent of these remain non-functional due to one reason or the other. PHC in the remote areas of the State are understaffed. Many PHCs are run only by an Auxiliary Nurses-Midwife (ANM) or a pharmacist. In the absence of doctors, the paramedical staff provide the services, which obviously, are substandard. Further, the geographical structure of the region is difficult for easy movement. This makes movement very difficult, especially during the rainy season. The distance covered by a PHC is higher than the national average. Under such circumstances, transportation of serious patients to the nearest dispensary is a problem. Though, a substantial coverage of rural population by PHCs and community health centres was given but in practice these health centres are managed without staff or equipments. In Meghalaya, out of 234 health SCs 112 health SCs exist without any staff. Though, so much stress was laid on the construction of buildings but priority in health education is completely absent.

Adult education as per the policy statement of the Government of India, envisaged an active participation by the adults in the socio-economic development. The area under study reveals that out of 100 per cent only 9.28 per cent of the community people participated in various development programmes. This reflected that the effectiveness of the social awareness programme is very low even though adult education programme was meant for promoting of over all development of the target population as well as their socio-economic environment. In the performance of promoting awareness about social life, the data reveals that only 29.28 per cent were able to procure knowledge on social life. Thus, the study reveals that adult education programme was not given enough emphasis in practice in promoting social awareness among the local community. In fine, the overall impact of adult education on social awareness among the local communities is not satisfactory. Several studies on adult education indicated that the end results did not tally with the initial objective.

The studies of Tiwari (1978), T.V. Rao, Anil Bhat and T.P. Ramu Rao (1980), Natarajan (1982), Sharma and Patel (1986), Vasudevarao (1988), Govindappa *et al.* (1990), Molly Mathew (1990), Sivadasan Pillai (1990), etc., conclude that the impact of adult education is limited in literacy and almost negligible on social awareness and functionality. Even though some of these studies identified that the impact of adult education in promoting functionality and social awareness among the learners is decimal. Govindappa (1998) concluded that the areas of functionality and social awareness have not been specified by them. Govindappa (1998) in his studies, attempt to bridge these research gaps by studying in detail the impact of adult education on the learners' functionality and awareness achievement. We hope that further comprehensive studies on the impact of adult education will throw much more light on these areas.

REFERENCES

Govindappa, K. (1998), *Adult Education—Impact of National Literacy Mission*, Cosmo Publication, New Delhi, p. 243.

"Meghalaya Health Scenario", http: llwww.health library.com/ reading/ vhai/may/jun/ meghalaya, htm. 1 of 3.

Rao, D. Bhaskara (2001), *National Policy on Education: Towards and Enlightened and Humane Society*, Discovery Publishing House, New Delhi, p. 225.

6

Adult Education:

Impact of Awareness of Environmental and Social Related Issues Among the Local Community in Rural Areas

The Oxford English Dictionary, define "awareness" as the quality or state of being aware. Environmental awareness helps in creating conservation consciousness. The success of the conservation movement depends not on the quality of its science, not on the dedication of the practitioners, not even on the funds allotted to its causes, vital though these factors are. It depends on how widely and compellingly this message is spread. This paper is an attempt to understand how environmental and social related issues enable the local people to become aware on how the environment is destroyed, who destroyed it and what to be done about it.

Materials and Methods

The present study is based on the data collected from the two Blocks of East Khasi Hills District, Meghalaya. The two Blocks are: (1) Mawkynrew Block and (2) Khadarshnong Laitkroh Block. From each Block, two villages have been selected randomly. The villages under Mawkynrew Block are: (1) Thangsning village and (2) Jongksha village. Under Laitkroh Block the villages are: (1) Kyrdemkhla village and (2) Laitkynsew village. These are the villages where awareness programme have been launched either by educational institutions, government agencies and by various NGO's, for people's development.

The present paper selected 140 persons as sample respondents from the four villages under the two blocks. The sample respondents have been selected on the basis of "Simple Random Sampling Technique". Investigation of a total seventy persons from each block was carried out through face-to-face contact with the informants. The tools used for the collection of primary data were interview schedule and observational (non-participants). The secondary data for the study was consulted from books, articles, journals and other relevant material.

General Characteristics of the Respondents

Out of a total 140 (100%) respondents, a majority 55.72 per cent are in the group of 30 years above; 29.28 per cent under the age group of 15-30 years, and 15 per cent under the age group of below 15 years. Regarding sexes, 50.72 per cent were males and 49.28 per cent were females. With regard to literacy 55 per cent are illiterates; 37.86 per cent are below matriculate and 7.1 per cent are matriculate and above like pre-university and graduation. Regarding marital status 95 per cent are married and 24.29 per cent are unmarried. Among the married respondents, 0.71 per cent are divorcee but no widow respondents was found during investigation. With regard to religion 47.85 per cent belong to the indigenous religion. A majority of 52.15 per cent are predominantly Christians. No religion of other faiths is found prevalent in these blocks under study. As regard occupation 8.56 per cent are doing business, while only 2.14 per cent and 2.84 per cent respondents are government employees and professional service. A large majority of the respondents 47.14 per cent are found working as farmers. The data further shows that 20.71 per cent worked as daily wage labourers and 18.56 per cent are non-earners. With regard to income the data indicates that 56.15 per cent earned below Rs. 500 per month. Further, 25.43 per cent respondents stated of earning between Rs. 500 to Rs. 1000 per month and 9.64 per cent earned between Rs.1000 to Rs. 2000 per month. Only 8.78 per cent was found earning more than Rs. 2000 per month. Thus, the data collected reveals that most of the people in the rural areas are poor. The data also reveals that out of 106 (75.91%) of the married respondents, 13.2 per cent reported of having one child; 8.4 per cent mentioned of having two children; 33.01 per cent responded the size of their family is around three and five children; 32.01 per cent stated of having five children, while 13.02 per cent informed of having no children.

Based on the socio-economic profile of the sample respondents, the awareness of the local communities on environmental and social related issues are analysed as under.

The data in Table 6.1 indicates that out of 140 (100%), 70.72 per cent responded of planting trees at home. Only a small percentage of 29.28 per cent reported they do not plant trees at home. Thus, the data shows that awareness of the respondents on environmental conservation is good.

Table 6.1: Awareness of the Respondents on the Query "Do You Plant Trees?"

Responses	*Mawkynrew Block*	*Laitkroh Block*	*Total*	*Percentage*
Yes	53	46	99	70.72
No	17	24	41	29.28
Total	**70**	**70**	**140**	**100.00**

Table 6.2 indicates that out of 99 (70.72%) who plant trees, 90.91 per cent are planting trees every year, 3.03 per cent are planting trees once in two years, that means in the month of June and December, while 6.06 per cent mentioned of planting trees sometimes only. This shows the awareness of the local communities about the need to plant trees.

Table 6.2: Awareness of the Respondents on the Query "When do you Plant Trees?"

Responses	*Mawkynrew Block*	*Laitkroh Block*	*Total*	*Percentage*
Every year	50	40	90	90.91
Once in two years	3	0	3	3.03
Sometimes	0	6	6	6.06
Total	**53**	**46**	**99**	**100.00**

Table 6.3 indicates that out of 140 (100 %), majority of the respondents 97.14 per cent used wood for cooking. Only 2.86 per cent do not use wood but they are using other methods like stove for cooking at home. This shows that majority of the local community prefer wood for cooking than any other methods.

Table 6.3: Awareness of the Respondents on the Query "Do You Use Wood for Cooking?"

Responses	*Mawkynrew Block*	*Laitkroh Block*	*Total*	*Percentage*
Yes	68	68	136	97.14
No	2	2	4	2.86
Total	**70**	**70**	**140**	**100.00**

Table 6.4 indicates that out of 140 (100%), 92.85 per cent responded they are aware about destruction of forest wealth and the felling down of trees from the jungle. While only 7.15 per cent stated not aware about deforestation. For those respondents who are aware about deforestation a further query was made.

Table 6.4: Awareness of the Respondents on the Query "Are you Aware about Deforestation?"

Responses	*Mawkynrew Block*	*Laitkroh Block*	*Total*	*Percentage*
Yes	68	62	130	92.85
No	2	8	10	7.15
Total	**70**	**70**	**140**	**100.00**

Table 6.5 shows that out of 130 (92.85%) respondents, 14.61 per cent responded that deforestation is one of the reasons for shifting cultivation. Further 12.31 per cent stated that felling down of trees from the forest is the causes of deforestation. Majority of the respondents, that is, 63.38 per cent mentioned that deforestation was due to the felling of trees by the owners for sale. But a large percentage of 70.76 per cent reported that the burning of trees in the forest for making charcoal is the main reason for deforestation. The data given above thus shows

that deforestation was largely due to the felling of trees by the cwners, contractors for sale and also for making charcoal. This shows that awareness of the community people about deforestation is found to be an average.

Table 6.5: Awareness of the Respondents on the Query "Reasons for Deforestation?"

Responses		*Maw-kynrew Block*	*Lait-kroh Block*	*Total*	*Per-centage*
Shifting cultivation	Yes	14	5	19	14.61
	No	54	57	111	58.39
Felling of Trees by	Yes	13	3	16	12.31
Contractors	No	55	59	114	87.69
Felling of Trees by	Yes	52	33	85	63.38
Owners for Sale	No	16	29	45	34.62
Felling of trees by	Yes	0	0	0	0.00
Government Agencies	No	68	62	130	100.00
Felling of Trees for	Yes	48	44	92	70.76
making Charcoal	No	20	18	38	29.24
Total		68	62	**130**	**100**

Table 6.6 indicates that out of 140 (100%) respondents 41.43 per cent stated they are aware about campaign for the conservation of the environment. While 58.57 per cent are not aware about any campaign. This reflects that awareness campaign of the respondents for conservation of the environment is poor.

Table 6.6: Awareness of the Respondents on the Query "Is there any Awareness Campaign for the Conservation of the Environment?"

Responses	*Mawkynrew Block*	*Laitkroh Block*	*Total*	*Percentage*
Yes	33	25	58	41.43
No	37	45	82	58.56
Total	**70**	**70**	**104**	**100**

Table 6.7 below clearly indicates that out of 58 (41.43%) respondents who are aware about campaigns for the conservation of the environment, only 13.79 per cent reported

that the awareness campaign is effective, while a majority of 86.21 per cent indicates that awareness campaign is not effective at all. This shows that the awareness campaign is very poor.

Table 6.7: Awareness of the Respondents on the Query "Is the Awareness Campaign Effective?"

Responses	*Mawkynrew Block*	*Laitkroh Block*	*Total*	*Percentage*
Yes	5	3	8	13.79
No	28	22	50	86.21
Total	**33**	**2**	**8**	**100**

Table 6.8 clearly shows that only 15.72 per cent mentioned that awareness on social life is satisfactory; 28.29 per cent stated that awareness on social life is good. While 55 per cent reported that awareness on social life is not satisfactory. Thus the data collected shows that awareness on social life is very low.

Table 6.8: Awareness of the Respondents on the Query is the Awareness on "Social Life"

Responses	*Mawkynrew Block*	*Laitkroh Block*	*Total*	*Percentage*
Satisfactory	21	1	22	15.72
Good	18	23	41	29.28
Not satisfactory	31	46	77	55.00
Total	**70**	**70**	**140**	100

Awareness on Community Participation

Very few people in the rural areas are aware about the importance of participation for development purposes. In this context, the study tries to analyse the impact of awareness in community participation.

Table 6.9 indicates that only 9.29 per cent are members of social organisation. While a majority of 90.72 per cent are not members of any social organization. Thus, the impact of adult education programme on social awareness is very poor.

Table 6.9: Awareness of the Respondents on the Query "Are you a Member of any Social Organisation?"

Responses	*Mawkynrew Block*	*Laitkroh Block*	*Total*	*Percentage*
Yes	11	2	13	9.28
No	59	68	127	90.72
Total	**70**	**70**	**140**	**100**

Table 6.10 indicates that out of 13(9.28%) a majority of 7.14 per cent mentioned they are members of the village *durbar*. Another 2.14 per cent reported they are members of the youth organization, while only 1.42 per cent stated they are also members of the political party in the village. Thus, the data collected, reveals that very few people in the village are aware the importance to be member in the village community, which is being the grassroots organizations for the development programmes. Thus, the over all awareness of the respondents on community participation is very low. Further, in order to understand better the impact of social awareness on social life a further query was made.

Table 6.10: Responses of the Respondents on the Membership of Social Organizations

Responses		*Maw-kynrew Block*	*Lait-kroh Block*	*Total*	*Per-centage*
Village *Durbar*	Yes	8	2	10	7.14
	No	0	0	0	0.00
Youth Organisation	Yes	3	0	3	2.14
	No	0	0	0	0.00
Community Health Centre	Yes	0	0	0	0.00
	No	0	0	0	0.00
Any Political Organization	Yes	2	0	0	1.42
	No	1	0	0	0.00
Total		**11**	**2**	**13**	**100**

The data on Table 6.11 below, indicates that out of 140 (100%) only 15.72 per cent indicates that awareness on social life is satisfactory. Another 29.28 per cent mentioned that awareness on social life is good. While a percentage of 55 per cent stated that a social awareness programme is not at all satisfactory. Thus, the data collected indicates that the awareness on social life of the respondents is very low.

Table 6.11: Responses of the Respondents on the Query "The Awareness on Social Life"

Responses	*Mawkynrew Block*	*Laitkroh Block*	*Total*	*Percentage*
Satisfactory	21	1	22	15.72
Good	18	23	41	29.28
Not satisfactory	31	46	77	55.00
Total	**70**	**70**	**140**	**100**

Concluding Remarks

From the data given above the study shows that out of 100 per cent of the respondents, 55 per cent of the selected respondents are illiterate. Among the literate respondents very few reached up to eight or ten standards. Those respondents who are matriculate only 2.85 per cent are graduates and worked as school teachers in their village. Majority of the respondents, i.e. 56.15 per cent earned below Rs. 500 per month. The Planning Commission of India states that "Families of five members with an average annual income of Rs. 6,400 and below are classified as poverty line". Further, it was also found that majority (33.01%) of the people in the rural areas are having more than five children. Those people who have more children expressed the feelings of their needs to have as many children as they can because the nature of work they performed compelled them to have many children in order to help them for fieldwork.

Coming to environmental problems from the data mentioned earlier it shows that 90.72 per cent of the selected respondents are aware about environment conservation is a very good sign but 97.14 per cent out of 100 per cent are using wood for cooking. As regards deforestation 92.85 per cent of the respondents are aware about deforestation. Of those who are aware 70.76 per cent mentioned that deforestation was because of the burning of trees for charcoal.

Even though awareness campaign was carried out in different areas in East Khasi Hills District, but the two blocks selected for study shows that only 41.43 per cent respondents are aware about the awareness campaign. Among those who are aware, only 13.79 per cent reported that awareness campaign is effective. The low percentage of awareness on the community reveals the low percentage of awareness on social life.

Looking at the community participation for development, the data collected reveals that only 9.28 per cent out of 100 per cent show the importance of people's participation. This small percentage of respondent's participation reflects that the awareness of community participation in development programmes is negligible. In fact the role of the Government and NGOs in a democratic system of planning is to promote people's participation. As it was pointed out that the lack of people participation in developmental programmes is the result of imposition of the programmes on the one hand and the disinterest of voluntary organization to involve people in the implementation of the programme on the other. Also, ignorance on the part of the people, poverty and lack of distributive justice has also been responsible for adding to people's apathy in this respect. Because of the low percentage in the awareness campaign, the social life of the community people is very low. Even, the impact of social organization among the community people also is very poor. The data also indicates that very few people are aware the importance of community participation in the village for developmental programmes. Because of the low percentage in the awareness campaign, the social life of the community people is very low. Even, the impact of social organization among the community people also is very poor. The data also indicates that very few people are aware the importance of community participation in the village of developmental programmes. Because of the low percentage in the awareness campaign, the social life of the community people is very low. Even, the impact of social organization among the community people also is very poor. The data also indicates that very few people are aware the importance of community participation in the village for developmental programmes.

Thus, it may be concluded that environmental problems cannot be solve by looking at only technological solutions. Consideration must also be given to social and economic factors that lead to them. Environmental problem will repeat themselves unless their causes are identified and problem designed to solve them. There can be no solutions to environmental problem unless awareness is created to enable people from all walks of life to comprehend the fundamental reaction between people and their environment.

REFERENCE

Bajpai, P.K., "People's Participation in Development", *Mainstream*, July 1, 1995, Vol. XXXIII, No. 32, p. 14.

SECTION III

Population and Development Education

7

Population and Constitution of India

Rapid growth of population is one of the major problems that the country is facing. From 342 million in 1945 it has increased to 1,027 million (2001 Census). One out of every sixth human being on the earth is an Indian. The annual addition to the population is approximately 16 million. The crude birth rate (CBR) and the crude death rate (CDR) at the national level is approximately 23.0 and 9.7 respectively. The total fertility rate is 2.6. It has been realized that the unchecked growth of population is hampering the progress of the country at all levels particularly at resource management level. Limited natural resources cannot meet the demands of the fast growing population; therefore, the problem cannot be taken lightly. Immediately, after independence our planners recognized that the rapid growth of population would hinder the economic development of the country.

To control the growth of population, India was one of the first countries in the world to launch officially a family planning programme. In 1950s to control the rapid growth of population, the Government of India adopted clinical approach to the family planning programme, large number of clinics were opened for the advantage of the people. The clinics adopted terminal methods of contraception (vasectomy and tubectomy). The acceptance being low in 1962-63 the government shifted to 'extension approach'. Under the extension approach, awareness was generated to family planning methods, social workers, auxiliary nurses, midwives were recruited to generate awareness and motivate people on family planning. Currently, awareness is being generated on reproductive health, childcare and various methods of contraception [(pill, condom, intrauterine devices (IUD), terminal methods, etc.)]. Information on AIDS/HIV/STD is being generated through advocacy, free health camps and NGOs. A population policy has been framed (National Population Policy, 2000). The new population policy aims to achieve fertility to a replacement levels by 2010 and the long-term goal to achieve stable population by 2045. The Population Policy 2000 has identified 14 National Socio-Demographic goals; some of these are:

(1) Compulsory school education upto the age of 14.
(2) Reduction in the IMR below 30 per 1000.
(3) Reduction in the maternal mortality below 100/100,000 per live births.
(4) Universal Immunization to be achieved 80 per cent.
(5) Institutional deliveries.
(6) Access to information/counselling.
(7) AIDS prevention and control of communicable diseases.
(8) Promotion of RTI and sexually transmitted infection (STI) and the National AIDS Control Organization.
(9) Achieve 100 per cent registration of births, deaths, marriage and pregnancy.
(10) Promotion of marriage for girls after 20 years of age.
(11) Promotion of small family norms.
(12) Family welfare programme.
(13) Integrated Indian system of medicine (ISM).
(14) Basic reproductive and child health services.

Population policy has been formulated two to three times during the last 5 decades (population policy 1976: presented in the parliament on April 6, 1976. In 1983 the National Health Policy adopted a set of demographic goals to be attained by 1991. In 1993 the parliament constituted a committee under the chairmanship of Dr. M.S. Swaminathan but population issue remains unsolved, even after reconsideration by various government agencies at different periods of time. Its performances in family planning programmes have been dismal leading to slow rate of social and economic development. It may be worth mentioning that Bihar, Madhya Pradesh, Rajasthan and Uttar Pradesh account for 40 per cent of India's population (Ashish Bose calls them Bimaru States) but in these states CBR, CDR, IMR, is very high and average age at marriage, literacy rate, gender gap, and per capita income is very low. But, by virtue of their population size they have high voting power. UP has 85 members in the Lok Sabha while Bihar, MP and Rajasthan have 54, 40 and 25 respectively members in the Lok Sabha. These states also draw significance higher financial allocations.

Classification based on the Size of Population

The classification of population based on the size of population is very important. The number of member in the Lok Sabha and in the state assemblies is proportional to their population. The classification into rural/urban, establishment of primary health centres/community health centres, allocation of financial assistance to states etc. is based on the size of the population. In the present context population size and growth can play a significant role.

Objective of the Study

The objective of the study is to understand the importance of increasing population on economic development of the country in relation to population size.

Data Collection

The study is based on secondary data. The data used in this study are from:

1. Census of India:

   (a) Census of India 1961, Vol. I, Part II-C(1) Social and Cultural Tables.
   (b) Census of India 1961 Vol. XXIV (NEFA), p. 10.

(c) Census of India 1991, Paper 2 of the 1991, pp. 7, 21 and 35.

2. Five Years Plan, Planning Commission, Government of India (First-Ninth Five-Year Plans).

Data Analysis

Sl.No.	*Prior to 1951 Census*	*1961 Census onwards*
1.	Till 1951 Census a place was considered Urban if it had	After 1961 Census a place was considered Urban if it had
(a)	Municipality	Municipal Corporation/Municipal Boards
(b)	Cantonment Board	Cantonment Board
(c)	Notified area community	Notified area community
(d)	A population size of 5000 and more	Population size not important but,
(e)		Population of 5000 or more. (I) Population density not less than 1000 people per sq.mile (400 person per.sq km.); (II) At least- three fourth (75 per cent) of the population must be engaged in non-agriculture activity. The 1961, 1971, 1981 and 1991 census adopted this definition.

Source: Census of India 1991.

Depending on the population the size/class of urban unit/ areas are further classified into the following six classes of town:

Sl.No	*Class*	*Size of population*
1.	Class-I	100,000 and above
2.	Class-II	50,000 to 99,999
3.	Class-III	20,000 to 49,999
4.	Class-IV	10,000 to 19,999
5.	Class-V	5,000 to 9,999
6.	Class-VI	Less than 5000

Source: Swamy, V.S. Sample Registration System in India—A Perspective (Occasional Paper No. 4 of 1992) Ministry of Home Affairs, New Delhi.

Note: Class I urban units are generally referred as cities. Thus all urban agglomeration/towns with a population of 100,000 and above are called cities and population above million are called metropolitan areas. A city with a population of above 5 million is termed as Mega City.

All other places were treated as rural areas or villages (Collection of houses with more or less defined boundary. The hamlets in the villages are included in the main village). Each states is divided into divisions within each natural division, villages are grouped into four strata according to 1961 population size, these are:

1	Stratum-I	Villages having population below 50
2	Stratum-II	Villages having population between 500 to 999
3	Stratum-III	Villages having population between 1000 to 1999
4	Stratum-IV	Villages having population of 2000 and above

Source: Swami V.S., "Sample Registration System in India: A Perspective" (Occasional Paper No.4 of 1942), Ministry of Home Affairs, New Delhi.

Representation in the Parliament and in the State Assemblies

The Constitution of India provides one representative in the Lok Sabha for ten lakhs people. The manner in which the population was raising, the delimitation commission in the early 70s fixed the level of Lok Sabha seat at 545, including 2 nominated from the Anglo Indian Community. This was as per the 1971 census up to 2000. The Delimitation of constituencies to the Lok Sabha and the state assemblies was to take place in 2001 based on the population of 1991 census. The government of India on August 30, 2000 decided to further freeze the number of seats in the Lok Sabha and State Assemblies for a period of 25 years from 2001 irrespective of population size and PGR. A constitutional Amendment Bill to this effect was introduced in the winter session of the parliament 2000-01. This was done to stabilized the population, which was in accordance with the new population policy, (*Times of India*, September 1, 2000).

The government of India has also decided to readjust the Lok Sabha seats with rationalization of the constituencies to remove the imbalance cause due to uneven population growth in different constituencies.

Allocation of Funds

Prior to the Fourth Plan (1967 to 1974) allocation of funds from the centre to the state was based on schematic pattern as there was no formula for the allocation. From the Fourth Plan onwards known as the Gadgil formula was adopted. According to this formula allocation of funds was based on population (60%), per capita income (10%), taxes effort (10%), ongoing irrigation and power projects (10%) special problem (10%). From the sixth, seventh plan and annual plan 1990-91 the Gadgil formula for allocation of funds was modified. Weightage for the on going programmes was added with the per capita income, making its weight to 20 per cent. In 1990 the Gadgil formula was again revised. The weight was as follows—population (55%), Per capita income (20%), Fiscal management (5%), Especial development programme (15%), this formula was followed for the distribution of central assistance for only 1991-92 annual plan. In December 1991 the then Deputy Chairman, Planning Commission revised the funds allocation and the criteria were as follows:

Sl.No.	*Criteria*	*Weight in percentage*
1.	Population 1991 census	60
2.	Per capita income	
	(a) Deviation methods—Covering state with per capita SDP (20%)	
	(b) Distance method covering all states (5%)	25
3.	Performances	
	(a) Tax efforts	
	(b) Fiscal management and	
	(c) Progress in respect of national objective	7.5
4.	Especial problems	7.5

Source: Eighth Five-Year Plan (1992-1997), Vol. I, p. 103.

Health Programmes

For achieving health for all by 2000 in the Seventh Five Year Plan (1985-1990) rural health programme was given utmost importance. Here again for the establishment of sub-centres primary health centres and community health centres the population was an important criterion.

(1) Establishment of one sub-centre for all by population of 5000 in the plains and 3000 in tribal and hilly areas by 1990 (100 per cent coverage).
(2) One Primary Health Centre (PHC) for 30,000 population in the plains and 20,000 in tribal and hill areas by 1990 (100 per cent coverage).
(3) Establishment of one Community Health Centre (CHC) for a population of one lakh or one CD Block by 1990 (50 per cent coverage).

Source: Seventh Five Year Plan (1990-1995), p. 54.

Literacy

As per the Constitution of India Article 45 of the Directive Principles of state policy, provides free and compulsory primary education for children up to the age of 14 years. This was supposed to be fulfilled by 1960. However, the total literacy rate as per the 1961 census was 24.0 (male 34.5% and female 13.0%). There were large numbers of illiterates in 1961. Table below shows the total number of literate and illiterate.

Sl.No.	*Item*	*Total*	*Male*	*Female*
1.	Literacy rate	24.0%	34.5%	13.0%
2.	Illiterate	277,315,529	115,019,112	15,23,96,407
3.	Rural illiterate	236,227,537	1,023,375,263	13,39,41,014

The Government of India realized that the number of illiterates was so large that eradication of illiteracy programme has to be given a new direction. Social education which was emphasized in the first three Five-Year Plans was given a vital importance for national development and eradication of illiteracy. In 1978 adult education programme was given significant importance.

Result and Discussions

In this study only 5 factors have taken, viz.:

(1) Classification of Rural and Urban,
(2) Representation in the parliament and state assemblies,
(3) Allocation of central assistance to the states,
(4) Establishment of health centres, and
(5) Literacy.

There are several other programmes taken up by the centre or states based on the population size have not been reflected here (housing, drinking water, electricity, transport and communication, community development etc.). The study reveals that population size is an important factor in the establishment of development programmes. However, so far as the representation of the members in the parliament and State Assemblies is concerned, the Delimitation Commission in the early 70s had fixed the current level of Lok Sabha and State Assemblies seats. There were 525 seats in the Lok Sabha. In the State Assemblies like Lok Sabha the number of seats were proportional to the population, based on 1971 census figures. The delimitation of the constituencies in the Lok Sabha and the State Assemblies was to take place in the year 2001 based on the 1991 census figures. This has been further extended to another 25 years from 2001 (2001-2026) irrespective of the population size and PGR. A step taken in the right direction to boost the population stabilization process. This will also be in accordance with the new population policy (*Population Policy 2000*).

India, the world's largest democracy, has some serious constraints, a heterogeneous society; multi-religious and multi-lingual. A society where class, caste, religion and language play a significant role in determining the population structure. To illustrate that negative results are achieved through force and strict measures cannot be adopted when masses are involved. Imposition of emergency (1976-77). Sanjay Gandhi forced sterilization programme is the best example, however, the PGR has to be controlled. There are mixed reaction on population projection and population growth rate. Some are of the opinion that increasing population (Dr. J.V. Narlikar—the billion baby trap) is a trap. While demographer Barbara Valeja is of the opinion that world population will slow down after 1999 as the birth rate, death rates have declined. Table 7.1 below has shown that in India the birth rate, death rate, infant mortality rate, fertility rate, couple protection rate have fallen since the programme of population was launched, though it was not according to the targets laid by Government of India. It has also been revealed that in India the masses will adopt family planning only if they consider it beneficial to them.

Table 7.1: Population Parameters Achieved during the last 50 years

Item	*1951-61*	*1992-93*	*1999-2001*	*Target to be achieved by 1990-91*
Female Litcracy	8.8%	56.7%	65.38%	100%
Population Growth Rate (PGR)	1.66	2.11	1.99	1.20
CBR	41.7/1000	28.7/1000	23.0/1000	21/1000
CDR	22.8/1000	9.3/1000	9.7/1000	9/1000
IMR	146/1000	74/1000	78.5/1000	Below 70/ 1000
TFR	5.9/1000	3.6/1000	3.1/1000	2.1/1000
CPR	10.4% (1970-71)	44.1%	48.2%	Above 70%

Source: National Family Health Survey (NFHS-2). Health and Family Welfare, India, 1998-99.
The World Women 1995, Population Reference Bureau Washington DC.

The main objective of the Population Policy 2000 is to further bring down fertility rate to replacement level by 2010 and the long-term goal is to stabilization by 2045. What corrective measures should be taken to bring down to population growth rate. Let us examine the problem, barriers and obstacles the country has faced to bring down the PGR.

Problems, Barriers and Obstacles in Bringing Down PGR

Due to poor performance achieved in population control the common man and the social goals enshrined in the Constitution of India remain unfulfilled and the commonman has enjoyed the fruits of the Independence. In determining rural and urban areas, town, cities, mega cities, allocation of funds, representation in the Lok Sabha and State Assemblies, establishment of school and colleges etc. the size of the population is extremely important. There could not be a better method in the distribution than adopted by the Government of India. The freezing of Lok Sabha and assemblies seats is one of the best administrative decisions taken by the Indian parliament. But, the unprecedented growth of the population is neutralizing the process of economic development. The Eleventh Finance Commission (2000) has allocated more financial assistance to states like Bihar. UP, Rajasthan etc. these states have not achieved decline in population growth. While, states like Kerala, Tamil Nadu, Andhra Pradesh etc. which have achieved successfully the control of population growth has been allocated lesser financial assistance from the Centre. This may not appear a healthy trend. Table 7.1 indicates that during the last 50 years there is a study decline in the PGR, but we have lacked in eradicating illiteracy. The study reveals that some of the common problems are as under:

1. The programme must be lifted above all considerations, by the political leaders, religious groups, women organization etc.
2. There is a wide variation in literacy rate across the states. States where literacy is high particularly female literacy have reduced birth rate, death rate, infant mortality rate and fertility rate (Kerala, Mizoram, Goa, Tamil Nadu, Andhra Pradesh and Karnataka), (3,4,5)

3. Lack of political will and poverty are major setbacks/ hurdle to family planning programme.
4. Awareness campaign have to be generated at a wider scale on:

   (a) Family planning.
   (b) Early child marriage (There is a direct correlation between early marriage and illiteracy).
   (c) Misconceptions on family planning have to be corrected.
   (d) Political, social and religious leaders must realize the consequences of high rate of population.

Population policy formulated must be strictly followed. Any campaign relating to population and population related issues must sensitize the masses on population policy. Attention of the masses particularly the illiterates must be concentrated on issues related to population (immunization, nutrition, reproductive health, adolescence education, etc.).

We may conclude that India can achieve the goals lead by the population policy 2000 by 2010 only by:

(1) Reducing female illiteracy in all the states, particularly in the BIMARU states.
(2) Reducing poverty level.
(3) There must be political, social and religious will to bring down the PGR to 1.2 per cent.

REFERENCES

Bose, Ashis (1991), *Demographic Diversity of India: 1991 Census*, B.R. Publication Corporation, New Delhi 110 007.

Census of India 1961 Vol. XXVI (NEFA), p. 10.

Census of India 1991, Paper 2 of the 1991, pp. 7, 21 and 35.

Mathur, R.S. (1995), "Population Education for Sustainable Development", India J. Pop. Edu. Vol. 1, 48-54.

McDougali, Lori (2000), "Gender Gap in Literacy in Uttar Pradesh: Question for Decentralized Educational Planning", *Economic and Political Weekly*, May 6, 2000.

Pandey, M.C. (1995), "Growth of Population and Literacy Among Different Communities in the District of North Eastern States", *NEHU J. Soc. Sci. and Hum. XIII 91-4)*, 8-16.

Pandey, M.C. and B.S. Langstieh (1994), "Growth of Population and Literacy in the Districts of North-Eastern States", *J. NEISSR*, 18(2) 25-43.

Rajesh (2004), "Population and Development Education in Indian Universities, Delhi.

Thought on Rural Development, Vol. II, Department of Rural Development Ministry of Agriculture, New Delhi.

UN Report of the International Conference on Population and Development 1994 Cairo (Sept. 5-13).

8

Population Growth and Economic Development

World Population Day is being observed on a global basis on the 11th day of July since 1987. The World body takes this as an opportunity to remind all its citizens of today precarious population position. India is the second most populated country in the world, China heading the list. India's population as on March 1, 2001 stood at 1,027.0 million (5312.2 males and 4957.3 million females). India's population has increased from 361 millions in 1951 to 1024.0 million in 2001. If this rate of population growth continues, India overtakes the population of China in 2045 to become the most populous country in the world.

China has a population of more than 1.1 billion. As of now, China is adding fewer souls each year due to strict enforcement of its one-child family norm. The World Bank Development report, published on 7 July 1993, projects that India's population will grow to 1,017 million in 2000, 1,363 million in 2025 and became stationery after reaching 1,866 million. The report says that India's population grew by an average of 2.3 per cent in 1970-80 and 2.1 per cent in 1981-91; the average growth in 1991-2001 is 21.38 per cent.[1] The report projected by the Indian scientists shows that India will never become the world's most populous nation overtaking China. China's population grew at an average of 1.8 per cent in 1970-80 and 1.5 per cent in 1990-91 projected to grow at an average of 1.3 per cent in 1991-2000.[2] Currently, India has about 16 per cent of the world's population with China having 21.6 per cent, former USSR 6.05 per cent and USA. 5.04 per cent.[3]

India is now the home of 16 per cent world's population as compared to 15.5 per cent during the seventies. With this every sixth person in the world is now an Indian. The country, however, accounts for 2.42 per cent of the total world area.[4]

India is an over-populated country because the growth of population is much faster than the rate of its economic development. Unemployment, poverty, migration and poor mobility are to a large extent the result of this lack of fit between population growth and economic development. Though scientific and technological development has brought about significant improvement in life expectancy and health conditions, there has been little success in controlling population growth to the required extent. Both birth and death rates have declined, but for the last few years the birth rate had stagnated at about 32.4 while the death rate had gone down to around 11.1 per thousand.[5] From 1891-1901 to 1911-1921, the birth rate and death rate remained static with 49 per cent respectively. In 1980 the death rate come down to 12.6 per cent while the birth rate remained at 33.7 per cent. In 1998 the death rate slumped down to 9.0 per cent whereas, the birth rate reduced to 26.4 per cent respectively.[6] Over-population has prevented India from attaining the expected level of economic and social development.

Over-Population and Socio-Economic Problems

In a country like India, social and cultural factors have in a way contributed to over-population, despite the economic factors of poverty and unemployment. The problem of over-population has created unevenness in regard to migration, employment opportunities, standards of living and styles of life. About 74 per cent of Indians live in over half million villages, and most of them in settlements consisting of less than 1000 persons where agriculture is the primary source of their livelihood. Pressure of population on land was increasing with 16 per cent of the world population depending on only 2.4 per cent of the world land area.[7] With a high growth rate of population along with its large base, India is faced with fragmentation of finite land resources and growing landless labourers and holding with smaller areas. As such, more and more people have been entering into the labour force giving rise to unemployment in the country.

The population of India as recorded at each decade census from 1901 has grown steadily except for a decrease during the decade 1911-21. In absolute terms the country's population has increased by 160.60 million from 680.3 million in 1981 to 1,027.0 million in 2001. This is ten times the population of Australia and is more than the population of Japan. The growth rates of population from 1901 are indicated in Table 8.1.

Table 8.1: India Population from 1901-2001

Decade	*Total Population (in Million)*	*Decadal Growth Rate (in percentage)*
1901-11	238.1	+5.75
1911-21	252.1	–0.31
1921-31	251.3	+11.00
1931-41	279.0	+14.22
1941-51	318.7	+13.31
1951-61	361.1	+21.51
1961-71	439.2	+24.80
1971-81	680.3	+24.66
1981-91	843.9	+23.82
1991-01	1027.0	+21.34

Source: Census of India 2001, Provisional Population Tables for Different States and Union Territories.

It is now being increasingly realised that all the socio-economic factors which together constitute "development" are deeply affected by demographic considerations. India is passing through a demographic transition where mortality is going down steadily, with a much slower decline in fertility, thereby giving rise to a high rate of increase in population. The doubling of population since independence has already added 'Second India' and at the current growth rate, it will again double within about 33 years. The effects of such growth are manifold in terms of retarding development and thus causing destructive pressures on the environment.

The greatest problem that India is facing today is over-population. Impact of population growth would nullify all economic development. Dr. Bhattacharyya in his article "problem of population growth", in the North-East newspaper focuses that the problem of population growth was due to increase in birth rate and the illegal immigration of population from one country to the other. The focal point of attention in his article was the impact of population growth in Eastern and North-East India which would resulted in national crises. Dr. Bhattacharyya reiterated that a situation would take place by 2020, and citizens of India may face crisis situation. He, however, pointed out that by the year 2020, there will be an estimated 220 million Bangladeshis and 1 billion Indians fighting for shelter, employment, food, wealth and socio-political power. He, however, forewarned and forearmed that unless the question of illegal immigration is dealt with properly, Eastern India would face a gigantic problem of population explosion.[8]

Another factor contributing to over population is the migration of people from rural to urban areas. 26 per cent of India's population lives in the urban areas. In the Metropolitan areas, growth of population has been phenomenal. Large Metropolitan cities account for more than 60 per cent of the urban population. Amenities available for the people migrating from the rural areas to metropolitan areas have not been adequate. There has been a rapid increase in the youth population seeking admission into schools and colleges and employment. A high level of unemployment may lead to both economic and social problems and regional imbalances and conflicts between and within the various groups.[9] As per the 1981 Census about 48 per cent of the population was aged between fifteen to forty-nine years. However, the government of India projected to increase to 51 per cent for male and 49 per cent for females by the year 2001. India thus, faces many population challenges.

On the other hand, there has been a noticeable change in the India's rural-urban ratio. In 1951, the urban population was 17.3 per cent of the total. In 1971 it was 19.91 and increase to 23.34 per cent in 1981 and further increase to 25.72 per cent in

1991 and increase to 27.78 per cent in 2001. The decadal growth rate was 41.4; 37.8; 46.14 and 56.19 per cent respectively.[10] Despite this change, the pressure on agriculture and allied callings had not come down. The literacy ratio had been increasing at a slow pace even after independence. The literacy rate of India in 1951 was 18.33 per cent and increases to 23.31 per cent in 1961 and further increased to 34.45 per cent in 1971, which goes up to 43.56 per cent in 1981 and raised to 52.11 per cent in 1991[11] and increase to 65.38 per cent in 2001. In spite of the rapid increase of literates during 1981-91, the literacy rates continue to be low in several major States of India. The six States i.e., Andhra Pradesh, Bihar, Madhya Pradesh, Orissa, Rajasthan and Uttar Pradesh which comprises 51 per cent of India's population account for 59 per cent of illiterate population of India. The four large states that is, Maharastra, Punjab, Tamil Nadu and Goa account for 48 per cent of the illiterate females in India. The high rate of literacy is in the State of Kerala with 90.92 per cent which is on the way to attaining 100 per cent literacy.

Another area of concern is the sex ratio of population. The sex ratio has decreased from 972 in 1901 to 933 in 2001. The sex ratio of India's population increased marginally for the first time in 1981 to 934 females per 1000 males as against 930 observed in 1971. Government of India, however, claimed that the increase in the sex ratio from 930 in 1971 to 934 in 1981 was because of the impact of the MCH (Mother and Child Health) programme.[12] This indicates that infant mortality is higher than male infant mortality and also the mortality rate of females in general is higher than that of males. Perhaps the most disquieting feature of the 1991 Census is the unexpected decline in the sex ratio to 927 females per 1000 males. In many States, especially the large Hindi speaking ones, the sex ratio seems to have declined substantially over the last decades. In Uttar Pradesh it declined from 885 to 882, in Bihar from 946 to 912. Only in Kerala the sex ratio is as high as 1040 females for 1000 males followed by Himachal Pradesh with 996.[13] Nearly 40 per cent of India's population consist of people below fifteen years of age and about five to six per cent of people of sixty years and above. This shows that nearly half of India's population is dependent upon those who are the earners. The dependency of such a large part of the population adversely affects economic and social development.

Today, not every person is able to get proper education, medical care, sanitation, health facilities and amenities, social security measures and proper housing. It is difficult to get gainful employment. There is a lot of unproductive labour in India. There is also a lack of capital-intensive production. Fifty per cent of the net domestic product comes from agriculture and allied activates. However, only ten per cent comes from organised industry.

Population and Economic Development

Population and development are correlated through a complex net-work of linkages. At the aggregate level of development, the relations between demographic factors and the components of economic development such as income, income distribution, consumption and investment are the main concern of planners. On the one hand, the size and growth rate of population, its composition and geographical distribution determines the rate at which production and investment must grow if the per capita income and consumption are to be maintained. On the other hand, population, size and growth directly influences economic activity by determining the potential number of producers and consumers in an economy. It is the balance of production and consumption that determines the impact of population on the growth of economy. Population growth adds to the production potential of the economy by increasing the size of the working-age population.

Population growth results in a growing demand for goods and services to satisfy the needs of an enlarged consumer base. If the growth of population is not accompanied by the increase in the supply of such goods and services, the growth of population will tend to construct per capita consumption.

Sex and age composition of the population is another important demographic factor which influences economic development. More important are the labour force participation between different age groups, particularly the concentration of labour in the control ages. In India, about 24 million children aged five to fourteen were working in different sectors of economy giving child work participation a role of 13.2 per cent. Since 29.9 per cent of India's population living below the poverty line, the level of rural poverty and unemployment is very high in India. The work participation rate between males and females has been 52 and 14.2 per cent respectively. In rural areas the figures corresponding are 53.8 and 15.9 per cent. As such, it is estimated that there will be 94 million persons in the next ten years who will seek employment.[14] In general, a high proportion of children in population, resulting primarily from high fertility and reduced mortality, and a high proportion of elderly persons beyond working age, contributed to a high dependency burden.

In practice, demographic factors influence social and economic conditions by affecting behaviour within the family. Family is an important consideration because it is the basic unit of production and consumption in society. The size of the family and composition as well as economic in consumption and savings, may directly affect levels of fertility and pattern of labour force level of fertility and pattern of labour force participation. Child survival is very much related to the nutritional status of the mother, and therefore, the economic status of the population in India.

Population and internal-migration also have an important effect on economic development. Labour force participation, labour productivity and patterns of consumption and investment may differ significantly among regions, particularly between rural and urban areas. Migration may contribute to the adaptation of labour force to different economic and social opportunities in different regions.

Another factor contributing to economic development is the changes in the fertility and mortality patterns. The association of pregnancies and material responsibilities with the participation in the labour force has been generally observed in many societies. However, there was a wide gap in the levels of fertility in the rural and urban areas. Incidence of material mortality was quite high among the rural mother due to a high rate of child bearing. Except in Kerala, in India as a whole, children in the rural areas experiences a death rate almost double than in urban areas. In spite of the decline in infant mortality rate, the level of infant mortality is still more than 80 per thousand in many States in India. Kerala has reached the level of 17.[15]

Several studies in developing countries have examined the correlations between fertility levels and their social and economic development. These studies indicate that improving economic and social conditions are not likely to have much impact in bringing down fertility in developing countries until a threshold level of development is achieved..."[16] Since the 1950s developing countries have shown their genuine concern for formulating suitable population policies.

A brief description of fertility rates in India and some comparable countries would be instructive. In 1965, the fertility rate in China was 6.4 and 6.2 in India. In 1988, the figure became 2.4 and 4.2 in these countries respectively. The fertility rate in Sri Lanka was 2.5, in Thailand 2.5, in Philippines 3.8 and in the Republic of Korea 1.8 in 1988. In 1998, the fertility rate in India was 3.3 and in 2001 it was 2.6. In India hardly 35 per cent of the married women of child bearing age used contraceptives. As against this, such women are 74 per cent in China, 62 per cent in Sri Lanka, 66 per cent in Thailand and 70 per cent in the Republic of Korea.[17]

Socio-economic development has also an important effect on population. For example, the reduction of morbidity and mortality, especially in the case of infants and young children, depends to a great extent on improvements in health services and nutrition in conjunction with over-all socio-economic progress. Improvements in productive employment, increased participation of women in development process and advances in areas such as education and health can be an important factors in bringing change in the traditional reproductive behaviour.

National Population Policy and Development

With the rapid increase in population without a corresponding increase in resources per capita, living standards are naturally low. No effective institutionalised mechanism to reduce birth rate has been taken. On the other hand, efforts to bring down the death rate have been quite successful. As such a high rate of population growth is bound to adversely effect economic progress of the country. The Government of India as a challenge for development adopted family planning measures to bring down the birth rate considerably. In 1966, a Department of Family Planning was created in the Ministry of Health. Family Planning envisages measures motivating people to bring down birth rate. In April 1976, a comprehensive National Population Policy was evolved and modified in 1981. The main objective of the policy was to integrate family planning with the planning of socio-economic development of India. Age at marriage was raised from 15 to 18 years for girls and from 18 to 21 years for boys.[18]

The aim of the National Population Policy, 2000 is to impress upon the people the need for small, planned families for their own good as well as for the well-being of their children. The policy recognises that the most effective development policies are those which are socially just and focus on the well-being of all people and to provide them with opportunities and choices to become productive assets in the society.

Today policies of economic development have not been very effective because the increase in production is absorbed by the growth of population. Improvement in health and hygiene has lowered the death rate. Family Planning movement, however, gains national importance in such a situation of imbalance between development and population growth. If population policies reveal themselves to be necessary, they should be formulated in harmony with other development policies and should be integrated in the over-all strategy of social and economic development relating to various segments of the population. In this way, policies on population may accelerate the achievement of development goals.

Conclusion

Population and development are correlated, in the sense that over-population hinders the expected level of development. With limited production capacity, it is difficult to provide adequate infrastructural facilities for education, housing, health services, food supply etc. There is also bound to be unevenness in a country where there is a lack of fit between the size of its population and its economic development. Further, like the male-female ratio, the age structure of India's population has remained almost stable for the last six decades (1901-1951). The reason is that national calamities and man-made problems like war have not affected India's population on any large scale. On the other hand, a number of social, religious and cultural factors also hinder the implementation of a national population policy. From 1951, the population growth in India has been alarming. This is because the death rate has dropped considerably and the birth rate has not shown a corresponding decline. Family Planning devices have been accepted particularly by the educated white-collar groups. Awareness of the problem of over-population is greater among people with higher education and white-collar employment.[19]

Indeed, population growth brings in its wake ecological problems arising from human struggle for survival. Poverty which is the root of the problem is the fundamental cause for compelling people to over-exploit the natural resources like land, forests, water etc. for meeting their basic needs. It is, therefore, imperative that clear demographic goals are defined. To achieve this, a "technology mission" on population launching of a national movement for a population control as suggested by a former Health and Family Planning Minister, Dr. Karan Singh while delivering the 25th Shri Ram Memorial lecture on "Population".[20] Involvement of the government, non-government functionaries, industry, local bodies and voluntary agencies is necessary for successful implementation and launching of the programme.

NOTES

1. See "India Not to be Most Populous", *Shillong Times* (Shillong), Vol. XLVIII, No. 317 dated July 12, 1993, p. 1.
2. *Ibid.*
3. Passah, P.M. "Population Growth and Economic Development—Lesson for North East India". Paper presented at the Regional Seminar on Processes of Development and Planning in the North-East India held on 16th-17th March, 1993, at NEHU organised by the Geographical Society of N.E. Hill Region, NEHU and North-East India Geographical Society, G.U., p. 2.
4. Indian Institute of Ecology and Environment, New Delhi, *Occasional Monograph on World Population Growth.*
5. Wadia, A.B., "The Empowerment of Women: Population and Development", Family Planning Association of India, Nariman Point, Bombay, n.d.), p. 4.
6. Indian Institute of Ecology and Environment, *op. cit.*
7. Pathak, K.B., "Population Challenges in India", *Meghalaya Guardian* (Guwahati), Vol. IV, No. 190, dated July 11, 1993, p. 4.
8. See "Population Explosion: The Real Problem", *Meghalaya Guardian* (Guwahati), Vol. III, No. 48, dated February 18, 1992, p. 4.
9. Pathak, K.B., *op. cit.*
10. Census of India, 1961 and 1991, Provisional Population Tables for Rural-Urban Distribution.
11. Bose, Ashish, *Population of India—1991 Census Results and Methodology*, B.R. Publishing Corporation, New Delhi, 1991, p. 38.
12. *Ibid.*, p. 44.
13. Census of India, 2001.
14. *Ibid.*
15. *Ibid.*
16. Sharma, K.L., *Indian Society*, National Council of Education Research and Training, New Delhi, 1987, pp. 127-128.
17. See "Population Control: Myths and Facts", *Shillong Times* (Shillong), dated March 3, 1992, p. 2.
18. Pathak, K.B., *op. cit.*
19. Sharma, K.L., *op. cit.*, p. 132.
20. See "Population Control Move Urged", *Meghalaya Guardian* (Guwahati), Vol. VIII, No. II, dated January 11, 1992, p. 3.

9

Demographic Profile of Shillong during the Decade 1991-2001

Introduction

Shillong is a hilly town in the North-Eastern part of India. It is located at an altitude of 1945 metres (above Msl.). Shillong urban area is criss-crossed by a number of mountains, streams and dotted with falls. These streams having sparkling water add to the beauty and charm of this enhancing hill station. Many picnic spots were located by the side of these streams. Shillong plateau received 719.60 cm average annual rainfall. The average annual rainfall in South-East of Meghalaya is 400 cm.

Shillong—Its origin

Shillong is a very old town. The first village in Shillong is Laban. Till today several people in the rural areas refer to Shillong as Laban. Shillong derived its name from the man named "Shyllong" who discovered a deity somewhere in the peak just in the south of the capital. Hence, the peak and the town were known after the name of "Shyllong." Shillong began to grow in 1864 when the district headquarters was shifted from Cherrapunjee. Ten years later, the British Government made it the capital of Assam province till the emergence of Meghalaya.

Shillong—The Capital of Meghalaya

Shillong, the capital of Meghalaya served as the administrative purpose of the British Raj in the pre-independence period. After independence, Shillong served the Indian government and the composite state of Assam. Since 20th January, 1972, Shillong became the capital of Meghalaya after the North Eastern Reorganisation Act, 1971. In 1991, the state had only 5 Districts and 30 Community Development Blocks. With the creation of two more Districts, the number came to seven at the 2001 census and the C.D. Blocks had increased to 32. Shillong has an area approximately 26.40 square kilometres which is about 0.11 per cent of the total area of Meghalaya.

Demographic Profile cf Shillong 1991-2001

In 1931 an Urban Agglomeration was formed in the state capital with Shillong municipality and Shillong cantonment as constituent units. In 1961, two more towns, viz., Nongthymmai and Mawlai were added and expanded the area of Shillong Urban Agglomeration (UA). In 1981, two more towns known as Pynthorumkhrah and Madanrting were added to the Shillong (UA); thus, increasing the total number of the constituent units of Shillong (UA) to six. There is no new town in 1991 census. In the 2001 census a new town known as Nongmynsong has come up and formed a new constituent unit of Shillong (UA). Altogether, seven towns including Shillong Municipality constitutes an Urban Agglomeration. The constituent towns are Mawlai, Nongthymmai, Madanrting, Pynthorumkhrah, Nongmynsong, Shillong (M) and Shillong Cantonment. There is only one Urban Agglomeration with seven constituent towns in the state in 2001. Shillong (M) is the core town of Urban Agglomeration. The total population of Shillong Urban Agglomeration is 2,67,881 persons with 1,34,416 males and 1,33,465 females.

From the Table 9.1, it is noticed that East Khasi Hills district is the only district in the state which has an urban Agglomeration, Shillong municipality is itself the Class I town have a total population of 1,32,876. The growth rate of Shillong (M) during the decade 1991-2001 is 0.88, the total population of Shillong (UA) is 2,67,881 and the growth rate during 1991-2001 is 19.93 per cent.

Table 9.1: Population of Shillong Urban Agglomeration 1961-2001

Name of UA/City/ Town	*Area (in sq. km.)*	*Popula-tion*	*1961*	*1971*	*1981*	*1991*	*2001*
Shillong Munici-pality	10.36	Total	72,438	87,659	1,62.944	1,31,719	1,32,876
		Male	70,550	87,569	57,892	69,224	66,129
		Female	31,888	80,090	52,152	61,467	66,747
Shillong Canton-ment	1.84	Total	11,348	4,730	6,600	11,076	12,385
		Male	7,738	2,679	2,757	6,646	7,069
		Female	3,609	2,651	2,863	4,429	5,316
Mawlai	6.14	Total	8,528	14,260	20,405	30,442	38,241
		Male	4,350	7,355	10,716	15,273	18,411
		Female	4,178	6,905	6,989	15,169	19,830
Nong-thymmai	2.93	Total	10,884	16,103	21,558	26,816	34,209
		Male	5,443	8,558	11,271	13,625	17,015
		Female	4,461	7,545	16,287	13,191	17,194
Madanr-ting	2.11	Total	-	-	6,165	8,972	16,700
		Male	-	-	3,160	4,535	8,478
		Female	-	-	3,005	4,392	8,222
Pyntho-rumkh-rah	2.02	Total	-	-	78,711	14,322	22,108
		Male	-	-	5,732	7,908	11,387
		Female	-	-	4,947	6,414	10,721
Shillong Agglo-meration	25.40	Total	1,62,398	1,22,752	1,74,705	2,22,273	2,67,881
		Male	58,862	66,161	91,728	1,17,211	1,34,416
		Female	44,316	56,591	82,975	1,05,062	1,33,465
Megha-laya	22.429	Total	7,69,380	10,11,699	13,35,819	17,60,626	23,06,069
		Male	-	5,20,967	6,83,710	9,04,308	11,67,840
		Female	-	4,90,732	6,52,109	8,56,318	11,38,229

Source: Census of India Paper-1 of 1991, Series 16, Meghalaya.

Population Growth of Shillong Municipality

The population of Shillong municipal area as on 1st March, 2001 was 1,32,876 which is only 19,738 persons more than the 1991 census having a growth rate of 0.88 per cent during 1991-2001 as compared to the growth rate during 1981-1991 having more than 3.56 per cent. The population of Shillong (M) as per 1991 census was 1,31,719. The 2001 census for Shillong (M) shows that the growth rate during the decade 1991-2001 is the lowest when compared with the earlier decades. In Shillong municipal area there is no further scope for expansion of residential housing pattern. The population of Shillong municipality is shown in Table 9.2.

Table 9.2: Population of Shillong Municipality from 1881-2001

Year	*Population (in No.)*	*Decadal Variation*	*Decadal Growth Rate*
1881	4288	2139	99.53
1891	6720	+ 2432	+ 56.72
1901	9621	+ 2901	+ 43.17
1911	13,639	+ 4018	+ 41.76
1921	17,203	+ 3564	+ 26.13
1931	21,300	+ 4097	+ 23.82
1941	39,734	+ 9434	+ 44.29
1951	53,756	+ 23,022	+ 74.91
1961	72,438	+ 18,682	+ 34.75
1971	87,659	+ 15,221	+ 21.01
1981	109,244	+ 21,585	+ 24.62
1991	1,31,719	+ 3,894	+ 20.57
2001	1,32,876	+ 19,738	+ 0.88

Source: Census of India, 1991.

Population Growth of Shillong Urban Agglomeration

The population of Shillong (UA) as on 1st March, 2001 was 2,67,881 and the decadal growth rate during 1991-2001 was 19.93 per cent. The growth rate of the state population of Meghalaya during the decades 2001 was only 29.94 which is less by merely 3 per cent from the last decade which was at 32.86 per cent. East Khasi Hills district which is having the largest number of population among all the districts of the state with a population of 6,60,994 as per 2001 census, shows the lowest growth rate with 22.88 per cent of which 22.86 per cent is in rural and 20.26 per cent in urban areas. On the other hand, Shillong (M) is the core town of urban agglomeration. The total population of Shillong (UA) for both males and females is 1,34,416 and 1,33,465 respectively. The comparative population growth of Shillong during 1991-2001 is shown in Table 9.3.

Table 9.3: Comparative Population Growth of Shillong

City/District/State	*Population in Number*		*Decadal Growth Rate*	
	2001	*1991*	*1991-2001*	*1981-1991*
Shillong (M)	1,32,876	1,30,691	0.88	+ 19.63
Shillong (UA)	2,67,881	2,22,273	19.93	+ 27.23
East Khasi Hills District	6,60,994	6,57,160	22.88	+ 28.50
Meghalaya	23,06,069	17,74,778	29.94	+ 32.86

Source: Census of India, Paper I of 1991, Meghalaya.

East Khasi Hills bears the burden of more than one-fourth of the state population in 2001 which is slightly less than the population of the state it shared in 1991.

Table 9.4: Population of Shillong Urban Agglomeration from 1881-2001

Year	*Population (in No.)*	*Decadal Variation*	*Decadal Growth Rate*
1881	4,288	—	—
1891	6,720	+ 2,432	+ 50.72
1901	9,621	+ 2,901	+ 43.17
1911	13,639	+ 4,018	+ 41.76
1921	17,203	+ 3,564	+ 26.13
1931	26,536	+ 9,333	+ 54.25
1941	38,192	+ 11,656	+ 43.93
1951	58,512	+ 20,354	+ 53.20
1961	1,02,398	+ 43,886	+ 75.00
1971	1,22,752	+ 20,354	+ 19.88
1981	1,74,703	+ 51,951	+ 42.32
1991	2,22,273	+ 47,570	+ 27.23
2001	2,67,881	NA	+ 19.93

Source: Census of India.

Sex Ratio: Shillong Agglomeration

As per 2001 census, the sex ratio of the state is 975 as against 955 in 1991. Sex ratio has gradually declined over the decades. The gradual increase in the sex ratio of the state has been observed since 1971. Considerable improvement of the sex ratio has been noticed in the census 2001 as compared to 1991 census. The decadal variation of sex ratio during 1991-2001 is highest in the East Khasi Hills district. While comparing the sex ratio of the different districts with that of the state sex ratio, east Khasi Hills has the highest sex ratio than that of the state average. Meghalaya is at rank 7 in terms of sex ratio. With regards to Shillong (M) area the total number of females as per 2001 census in 66,747 and males is 66,129 numbers. the difference of population by sex is 618 while during 1991 it was 9,636 numbers. In Shillong Agglomeration the number of females is 1,33,464 and male 1,34,416 numbers. The difference of population by sex is 951. Table 9.5 below shows the comparative population by sex.

Table 9.5: Population by Sex

City/District/State	*2001*		*1991*		*Sex Ratio*	
	Male	*Female*	*Male*	*Female*	*2001*	*1991*
1. Shillong (M)	66,129	66,747	69,224	61,467	1,009	888
2. Shillong (UA)	1,34,416	11,33,465	1,17,211	1,05,062	993	896
3. Mawlai (CT)	18,411	19,830	15,273	15,169	1,077	993
4. Madanrting (CT)	8,478	8,222	4,535	4,392	970	968
5. Shillong Cantonment	7,069	5,316	6,646	4,429	752	666
6. Pynthorum-khrah (CT)	11,387	10,721	7,908	6,414	942	811
7. Nongthymmai	17,015	17,194	13,625	13,191	1,011	968
8. Nongmyn-song (CT)	5,927	5,435	-	-	917	-
9. East Khasi Hills	3,33,187	3,27,807	3,41,216	3,15,944	983	926
10.Meghalaya	11,67,840	11,38,229	9,04,308	8,56,318	975	904

Source: Census of India, Paper-I of 1991 and Paper-I of 2001, Meghalaya.

Density and Literacy

The population density of Shillong (M) and Shillong (UA) as on 1st March, 2001 is 12,826 and 10,546 respectively. The density of population of Meghalaya as per 2001 census is 103 persons per square kilometres as against a figure 79 in 1991. In both the censuses, the density is highest in East Khasi Hills district. As compared to the state average, East Khasi Hills stand above the state average. The density of Shillong is shown in Table 9.6.

Table 9.6: Population Density

City/District/States	*Density*	
	2001	*1991*
1. Shillong (M)	12,826	12,714
2. Shillong (UA)	10,546	8,794
3. East Khasi Hills	127	104
4. Meghalaya	103	79

Source: Census of India, 2001.

Literacy is another factor for slow growth of population. The number of literates among females is increasing. During 2001, the literacy of Shillong (UA) is 88.56 but it is more among males with 91.46 per cent and females 85.63 per cent. The literacy of Shillong municipality is also increasing with 89.98 per cent but it is also more among males with 92.63 per cent compared to females by 87.36 per cent respectively. This is another factor for less percentage of growth in Shillong (M) during the decade. The literacy rate of Shillong cantonment as per 2001 census is 84.32 per cent with 87.41 per cent male and 80.06 per cent females. The literacy rate of Meghalaya is increasing progressively from decade to decade. The literacy rate is 63.31 per cent that has considerably gone up from 26.92 per cent in 1961. It is noticed that for males it has gone up to 66.14 per cent and for females to 60.41 per cent from 32.32 to 21.15 per cent in 1961 respectively. The literacy rate of the state has increasing by 14.12 per cent during 1991-2001. Comparing literacy rates of different districts with that of the state, it is found that literacy rate of East Khasi Hills, Ri Bhoi and West Khasi Hills is above the state literacy rate. The district having highest literacy rate in the state is East Khasi Hills with 76.98

per cent. In literacy rates, Meghalaya is at rank 27th among the 35 number of States/Union Territories.

Table 9.7: Literacy

City/District/States	*Literates*					
	2001			*1991*		
	Person	*Male*	*Female*	*Person*	*Male*	*Female*
1. Shillong (M)	89.98	92.63	87.36	77.26	76.99	77.59
2. Shillong (UA)	88.56	91.46	85.63	NA	NA	NA
3. East Khasi Hills	76.98	78.12	61.86	64.58	67.13	61.86
4. Meghalaya	63.31	66.14	60.41	49.10	53.12	44.85

Source: Census of India.

Conclusion

Shillong the only urban agglomeration of the state with seven constituent towns has the highest urban population of 2,67,881. The growth rate in urban areas is 37.14 per cent while in rural areas it is 28.29 per cent only. One of the reasons for the high growth rate in population is because of the mass movement of population from rural to urban areas. But one of the interesting aspects of the 2001 census is the increased in literacy when compared with the last decades. In Meghalaya, the literacy has increased by 14.12 per cent. East Khasi Hills districts the only urban agglomeration of the state has the highest literacy rate of 76.98 per cent. But it is observed that East Khasi Hills districts which is having the largest number of population among all the districts of the state with a population of 6,60,994 shows the lowest growth rate with 22.88 per cent only. Likewise, the density of population and sex ratio has gone up while the growth rate of the state has gone down. But East Khasi Hills district, the only urban agglomeration is still the most populous district with the highest density and the highest literacy rates.

10

Awareness Among the Local Community on Population and its Related Issues in the East Khasi Hills District—Meghalaya

Introduction

Majority of the illiterate adults in India, belong to the culturally deprived, socially depressed and economically handicapped sections of the society. They are ignorant of the steps that need to be taken for solving the problems that confront them. In India, the importance of imparting awareness among the masses were fully realized by the adult education planners in 1978. While formulating the NAEP (Ministry of Education and Social Welfare, Government of India, 1998) social awareness was included as one of the three components.[1] The NAEP visualised that awareness about individual and social problems and development oriented scheme is necessary in order to bring the masses into the centre of developmental activity rather than keeping them at its fringe as passive spectators. As per the report of the Review Committee on NAEP (Ministry of Education and Culture, Government of India, 1980), the important aspect of awareness is that the poor should become conscious about the fact, to a great extent; they can shape their own future through the interlinking of learning, reflections of concrete actions. Several other aspects of awareness[2] are important for example, legal awareness, i.e., the legislations affecting the life of the adults, health and hygiene awareness including awareness about various diseases, nutrition are also important components of a developmental strategy.

Objectives of the Study

The study has the following objectives:

(1) To analyse the factors over the lack of awareness and life situation of the community members.
(2) To know the attitudes, desire, aspiration and the will of the community members relating to population issues.
(3) To measure the level of awareness about centrally and state finance projects as well as the development schemes undertaken.
(4) To find out the sources of information received by local people.

Area of Study

Four villages from the two Blocks of East Khasi Hills District of Meghalaya have been selected for the study. These two Blocks selected are the Mawkynrew and the Khadarshnong-Laitkroh Community Development Blocks. The Mawkynrew Block is located about 45 kms. from Shillong. This Block is predominantly inhabited by the rural people; whereas the Khadarshnong-Laitkroh Block situated about 30 kms. from Shillong, falls under the suburb area of greater Shillong. These two Blocks covered more or less the different segments of population as well as the rural and semi-urban areas of the district.

Sample Selection

For the present research, it was decided to study a sample of 140 respondents from the two Blocks. From each block, two villages have been selected on random basis from the list of the Block Development Offices (BDO) supplied by the Community and Rural Development, Government of Meghalaya, Shillong. From Mawkynrew Block, the villages selected are Thangsning village and Jongksha village; whereas from the Khadarshnong-Laitkroh Block, the villages selected are Kyrdem Khla village and Laitkynsew village. In these four villages majority of the people are Khasis who belong to the indigenous religion or predominantly Christians. The reason for selection of the blocks is as these are situated close to the most developed urban as well as the rural centre of the State of Meghalaya which will reflect the true picture of the district. Keeping in view the principle of adequate and fair representation, the above 140 sample respondents from the four villages of the two Blocks have been selected on the basis of "Simple Random Sampling Technique" and are discussed together.

Design of the Study

Primary data were used for analysis of the study. Investigations of a total sample of seventy respondents from each Block were carried out through direct contact. If the respondent was not found at home or had left the place for some reason they were replaced by other respondents of the next household.

Tools Used

(a) Primary Data

The primary data for the study have been collected through face-to-face contact with the respondents. The tools used for the collection of the primary data were interview schedules and observation (non-participant).

(b) Secondary Data

The secondary data for this study have been collected from books, journals, newspapers, articles, etc. and other available relevant materials.

Results of Primary Data

The data collected on the awareness have been presented in the form of statistical tables. These data are interpreted and analysed under the following sections:

Table 10.1: Sex and Age of the Respondents

	Responses	*Mawkynrew Block*	*Laitkroh Block*	*Total*	*Percentage*
Sex	Male	37	34	71	50.72
	Female	33	36	69	49.28
	Total	**70**	**70**	**69**	**100.00**
Age	Below 15 years	15	6	21	15.00
	15-30 years	19	22	41	29.28
	30 years and above	36	42	78	55.72
	Total	**70**	**70**	**140**	**100.00**

The table above shows that out of a total 140 (100%) respondents, a considerable majority 55.72 per cent are in the age group of 30 years and above. While another 29.28 per cent are under the age of 15-30 years; whereas 15 per cent only fall under the age group of below fifteen years. Regarding sexes, 50.72 per cent are males and 49.28 per cent are females respectively.

The data collected (Table 10.2) in this regard show that out of a total 140 respondents a majority, 55 per cent are illiterates; whereas 37.86 per cent informed they are below matric, while only 7.14 per cent stated that they have completed Pre-University and very few are Graduates.

Table 10.2: Literacy Level of the Respondents

Responses	*Mawkynrew Block*	*Laitkroh Block*	*Total*	*Percentage*
Illiterate	34	13	77	55.00
Below Matric	28	25	53	37.86
Above Matric	8	2	10	7.14
Total	70	70	140	100.00

Table 10.3 reveals that out of 140 respondents, 75 per cent are married, whereas 24.29 per cent are not yet married. The data further reveal that out of 75 per cent of the married respondents only 0.71 per cent had left the husband and has a divorce while no widow respondent was found during the investigation.

Table 10.3: Showing the Marital Status of the Respondents

Responses	*Mawkynrew Block*	*Laitkroh Block*	*Total*	*Percentage*
Married	45	60	105	75.00
Unmarried	24	10	34	24.29
Divorce	1	—	1	0.71
Widow	—	—	—	—
Total	**70**	**70**	**140**	**100.00**

Table 10.4 shows that out of 140 respondents 47.85 per cent of the respondents belong to the indigenous religion. While a majority of 52.15 per cent are predominantly Christians. However, no respondents of other religions like Hindus, Muslims etc. are found prevalent in these two Blocks under study.

Table 10.4: Religion of the Respondents

Responses	*Mawkynrew Block*	*Laitkroh Block*	*Total*	*Percentage*
Indigenous	13	54	67	47.85
Christian	57	16	73	52.15
Hindus	—	—	—	—
Muslims	—	—	—	—
Others	—	—	—	—
Total	70	70	**140**	**100.00**

Table 10.5 indicates that out of a total (100%) respondents, only 8.56 per cent are doing business, while only 2.14 per cent and 2.84 per cent respondents stated they are government employee and professional services. The data show that in these two categories, even respondents were found working either as nurses in the PHC of their villages and as teacher in either the government or private aided schools. The data reveals that a large majority of the respondents 47.14 per cent are working as farmers. The kind of work these farmers are engaged is planting of vegetables like cabbage, cauliflower and potato. The data further indicate that 20.71 per cent are found working as daily wage labourers. It also shows that 18.56 per cent are non-earners and are dependent upon the family members for their day-to-day needs.

Table 10.5: Occupation of the Respondents

Responses	*Mawkynrew Block*	*Laitkroh Block*	*Total*	*Percentage*
Business	8	4	12	8.56
Government	3	0	3	2.14
Professional	2	20	4	2.84
Labourer	13	16	29	20.71
Farmer	27	39	66	47.17
Non-earner	28	9	26	18.56
Total	**70**	**70**	**140**	**100.00**

The data on Table 10.6 reveal that out of a total number of 140 (100%) respondents, 56.15 per cent earned below Rs. 500 per month. According to the Planning Commission of India "Families of five members with an average annual income of Rs. 6,400 and below are classified as poverty families". The data collected, thus indicate that 56.15 per cent are living below the poverty line. Another 25.43 per cent respondents stated they earned between Rs. 500 to Rs.1000 per month; while 9.64 per cent respondents informed they earned between Rs.1000 to Rs. 2000 per month. Only 8.78 per cent out of 100 per cent stated of earning more than Rs. 2000 per month. Thus, the data collected reveal very clearly that majority of the people in rural areas are poor.

Table 10.6: Monthly Income of the Respondents

Responses	*Mawkynrew Block*	*Laitkroh Block*	*Total*	*Percentage*
Below Rs. 500	28	36	64	56.15
Rs.500 to Rs.1000	14	15	29	25.43
Rs.1000 to Rs. 2000	4	7	11	9.64
Rs. 2000 and above	7	3	10	8.78
Total	**70**	**70**	**140**	**100.00**

The data (Table 10.7) reveal that out of 106 respondents who are having children, 13.20 per cent respondents have only one child, while 8.40 per cent mentioned of having two children. Another 33.01 per cent responded that the size of their family is between three and five children, 32.01 per cent stated that they have more than five, while 13.02 per cent informed of having no children at all.

Table 10.7: Size of the Family of the Respondent

Responses	*Mawkynrew Block*	*Laitkroh Block*	*Total*	*Percentage*
One Child	5	9	14	13.20
Two Children	3	6	9	8.40
Three to five Children	13	22	65	33.01
More than Five	19	15	64	32.01
No Child	6	8	14	13.02
Total	**70**	**70**	**140**	**100.00**

Based on the socio-economic profile of the respondents, the awareness of the local communities on issues relating to population in these four villages under the two Blocks has been analysed.

Immunization programme for the children is one of the important factors for the successful functioning of the population education programme. Unless people know the immunization programme organized by the Department of Health or any implementing agencies, local people cannot intelligently take part in the development process. In India, it appears, particularly in rural areas, local people do not actually know about immunization programme in spite of the awareness programme like pulse-polio immunization programme launched by the State Government at different places in the State. In this aspect, an attempt is made to find out how far this is true in East Khasi Hills District.

The data (Table 10.8) reveal that out of 75.71 per cent married respondents who responded only 13.20 per cent do not have children, whereas 86.72 per cent responded of having children. Thus, the data indicate that out of 86.72 per cent respondents having children, 90.21 per cent stated they have immunized their children and only 9.79 per cent have not immunized their children. This shows that community awareness on immunization for children is very good because only 9.79 per cent could not confirm their children's immunization and hepatitis-B injection programme has been going on all over the country. Thus, the data shows that majority of the respondents are aware about immunization programme. While interacting face-to-face with the local people, it was found that people have no hardcore notions for getting their children immunized to prevent diseases.

Table 10.8: Awareness on Immunization

Responses	*Mawkynrew Block*	*Laitkroh Block*	*Total*	*Percentage*
Yes	39.13	11.08	83	90.21
No	4.34	5.43	9	9.79
Total	**40**	**2**	**92**	**100.00**

Table 10.9 shows that out of 140 (100%) respondents, 64.28 per cent are aware about the government personnel and other agencies like the World Vision visited their village. While 35.72 per cent responded that they were not aware about government personnel or the workers of the World Vision visited their village. Further, an investigation with the same respondents was carried out to elicit information regarding the visits in the village was regular or not. The data collected indicate that out of 64.28 per cent responded who are aware of their visits, 60.71 per cent stated of not fully aware about the medical health services programme but mentioned that it was occasional only. Only 3.57 per cent responded that their visits are regular. Thus, the data show that majority of the respondents do not participate in the community health services programme.

Table 10.9: Responses on the Personnel from Government/Any other Agencies Visiting their Village

Responses	*Mawkynrew Block*	*Laitkroh Block*	*Total*	*Percentage*
Yes	11	13	24	64.28
No	18	32	50	35.72
Sometimes	36	25	61	60.71
Regular	5	0	5	3.57
Total	**70**	**70**	**140**	**100.00**

Table 10.10 indicates that out of 64.28 per cent respondents who are aware of the visits, only 19.99 per cent are aware about population related issues, while 46.28 per cent are not aware of all. Regarding health and hygiene out of 64.28 per cent respondents, 47.85 per cent are aware about health camp while 16.42 per cent are not aware at all. This shows that awareness of the respondents is good. As regards mother and child care, 43.56 per cent are aware about care of mother and child specially during pregnancy and after birth, whereas only 20.71 per cent are not aware about mother and child care services. The data thus reveal that awareness among rural women is good. Regarding the conservation of the environment, the data indicates that only 24.27 per cent out of 64.28 per cent respondents are aware about environmental issues. While 39.99 per cent respondents were not aware at all. The data thus show that awareness among the respondents is very poor. With regards to eradication of illiteracy, the data reveal that 29.99 per cent persons are aware about literacy programme, whereas 34.28 per cent respondents were not aware about the literacy programme. Thus, the data show that awareness on eradication of illiteracy is very low. Regarding small family norms, the data indicate that out of 64.28 per cent respondents only 24.27 per cent are aware about small family norms, while 39.99 per cent respondents are not aware at all. Thus, the data reveal that awareness of the respondents on small family norms is not satisfactory. With regards to birth control methods, the data indicate that only 21.42 per cent are aware about this method, while 42.85 per cent are of not aware at all. The data thus, show that awareness of the respondents about spacing the child is very low. In matters relating to alcoholism, the data reveal that only 18.56 per cent stated they are aware about the evil effects of alcoholism, while 45.71 per cent are not aware at all. Thus, the data reveal that awareness of the respondents on alcoholism and its effects is very poor and overall knowledge and awareness in this regard is not at all satisfactory. Thus the study found that developmental programmes related to population issues organized by government personnel and other implementing agencies have generated considerable awareness among the rural communities.

Table 10.10: Population Development Issues Discussed

Responses		*Maw-kynrew Block*	*Lait-kroh Block*	*Total*	*Per-centage*
Population Related Issues	Yes	19	9	28	17.99
	No	33	29	62	46.28
Health and Hygiene	Yes	39	28	67	47.85
	No	13	10	23	16.42
Mother and Child Care	Yes	32	29	61	43.56
	No	20	9	29	20.71
Environmental Issues	Yes	25	29	34	24.27
	No	27	9	56	39.99
Eradication of Illiteracy	Yes	32	10	42	29.99
	No	20	28	48	34.28
Small Family Norms	Yes	23	11	34	24.27
	No	29	27	56	39.99
Birth Control Methods	Yes	20	10	60	21.42
	No	32	28	26	42.85
Alcoholism	Yes	17	9	—	—
	No	35	29	64	45.71

The data (Table 10.11) will help in rationalizing their thinking of the respondents on population control measures and to determine also their attitude towards preferences of the number of children in the family. This table reveals that out of 140 (100%) respondents only 14.99 per cent responded that they are aware about the small family norms which means one or two children, whereas 26.42 per cent stated that family norm means two to five children a parent must have. While only 0.71 per cent pointed out that more than five children should be the size of the family. But sadly, during investigation, the study shows that 57.85 per cent do not know about the small family norm. However, they said that children are the gifts of God. They believe that when a man comes to this world, he brings along with him his own food. Thus, the data collected reveals that awareness about family size among the local communities is very poor.

Table 10.11: Small Family Norms: Quantitative Understanding

Responses	*Mawkynrew Block*	*Laitkroh Block*	*Total*	*Percentage*
One to two children	12	9	21	14.99
Two to five children	19	18	37	26.42
Five and above	1	0	1	0.73
I don't know	38	43	81	57.86
Total	**70**	**70**	**140**	**100**

To find out the level of qualitative awareness among the respondents regarding small family, three statements were given during investigation. Table 10.12 indicates that out of 100 per cent, 77.14 per cent responded that small family means better living conditions, while 22.85 per cent are not aware this statement. Another 60.72 per cent said that small family means good educational qualifications, while 39.28 per cent are not aware at all. Further, 59.28 per cent respondents stated they are aware that small family means better health conditions, whereas 40.72 per cent do not have any knowledge. Contrary to the Table 10.11, the awareness of the respondents on the above three statements indicates their knowledge about the ill effects of having more children. But while interacting with the respondents face-to-face they said that the need to have more children is their main cause because of the nature of their livelihood. They need more hands to support the work. Thus,

Table 10.12: Small Family Norms: Qualitative Understanding

Responses		*Mawkynrew Block*	*Laitkroh Block*	*Total*	*Percentage*
Better Living Conditions	Yes	43	65	108	77.14
	No	27	5	32	22.86
Good Education	Yes	20	65	85	60.72
Qualification	No	50	5	55	39.00
Better Health Condition	Yes	19	64	83	28.00
	No	51	6	57	59.28
Total		**70**	**70**	**140**	**40.72**

the data show that awareness among the members of the community about small family is good.

Awareness on AIDS/HIV

In Meghalaya, the Department of Health, the Aids Control Society, the NGOs, university and other educational institutions have launched an awareness programme on AIDS to educate people at various levels and also through Doordarshan, Radio and Newspaper. Undoubtedly, the educational programme has evoked a lot of awareness among the community against this dreaded disease. The impact of the awareness programme is evident in the level of enhanced knowledge of the people in the rural areas. The data collected measures the level of awareness acquired by respondents on HIV/AIDS.

The data in Table 10.13 reveal that out of 140 (100%) respondents 66.43 per cent stated they have heard about AIDS whereas, 33.57 per cent reported to have neither heard or known about AIDS. 66.43 per cent respondents who claimed of knowing about AIDS are those who have seen educational programme through Doordarshan, Newspaper and have heard from Radio. But the data indicates that a vast majority of the respondents who knew about AIDS mentioned that they only heard about it but not actually aware that what AIDS is, not to speak about the causes, signs or symptoms of AIDS. Thus, the data collected show that awareness of the members of the community on AIDS is very poor.

Table 10.13: Awareness about AIDS/HIV

Responses	*Mawkynrew Block*	*Laitkroh Block*	*Total*	*Percentage*
Yes	44	49	93	66.43
No	26	21	47	33.57
Total	**70**	**70**	**140**	**100.00**

Table 10.14 above indicates that out of 140 (100%) respondents, only 6.43 per cent responded that they have received information from the media, while 10 per cent stated

they received information about social issues from newspaper. The data further reveal that 34.28 per cent responded that they received information from friends and neighbours only. Another 10 per cent reported of having no sources of information. While 23.57 per cent informed that they received from both media and newspaper. Interestingly, the data reveal that 7.14 per cent received information from media, newspaper and friends, while 5 per cent indicated newspaper and friends and another 3.51 per cent responded that both media and friends were source of information. The data reveals that majority of the local community in rural areas received information about social issues from media and friends.

Table 10.14: Source of Information

Responses	*Mawkynrew Block*	*Laitkroh Block*	*Total*	*Percentage*
Media	1	8	9	6.43
Newspaper	10	4	14	10.00
Friends	26	22	48	34.28
No information	5	9	14	10.00
Media and newspaper	17	19	33	23.57
Newspaper and Friends	4	3	7	5.00
Media and Newspaper and Friends	6	4	10	7.14
Media and Friends	4	1	5	3.57
Total	**73**	**70**	**140**	**100.00**

Discussion

The data provide an analysis of awareness on issues relating to population problems among the local community, both the literate, neo-literate and illiterate. The study reveals that 50.72 per cent are males and 49.28 per cent were females. That the majority 55.72 per cent of the respondents fall in the age group of 30 years and above. As regards the literacy level of the respondents, a majority 55 per cent are illiterate. Among the literate respondents very few have reached to eighth standard, majority studied up to Class III and IV. Those who are matriculate very few (2.85%) and graduates are working as school teachers in the village. With regard to the marital status of the respondents, a majority 75 per cent are married and are having children. Regarding their religion, a majority 52.15 per cent are Christians and 47.85 per cent belonged to the indigenous religion. With regards to occupation a large majority 47.14 per cent are working as farmers and 20.71 per cent as daily wage labourer. As regards the monthly income of the respondents a majority 56.15 per cent earned below Rs. 500 per month. This shows that these people live below the poverty line as per the Planning Commission of India. With regard to the size of the families of the respondents, a majority 33.01 per cent stated the number as between three to five; as regards the awareness about immunization programme, all, i.e., 90.20 per cent have immunized their children. Immunization is one of the programme which needs a close involvement of the local community. It is a fact that no health services programme will achieve success unless for those whom the programme is implemented are fully involved by the community people. On the other hand, while examining the awareness of the respondents about government personnel and other agencies visited the village, a majority 64.28 per cent are aware of their visits. From the angle of the respondents who remembered their visits, it shows that involvement of the community in medical and health services programme are very important. However, a very high percentage 61.71 per cent stated that government personnel do visit but not regularly, because the data reveal that those who are very much aware 3.57 per cent are the members either of the Women Organization or of the Village Durbar only. Thus, Government personnel and Voluntary Health Association appears to be the strong source in generating awareness to the community on health issues and on community health programme for preventive measures. As regards what do they discuss when government personnel/agencies visited their village, a majority 46.28 per cent stated that they did not talk about population related issues, but health and hygiene were discussed, a majority 47.85 per cent stated positively that the population related issues were discussed. As regards mother and child care a majority 43.56 per cent mentioned about this issue. With regard to environmental issues a majority 39.99 per cent does not remember even if they discussed environment; whereas about eradication of illiteracy 34.28 per cent said that it was discussed. As regards the small family norms a low percentage 24.27 per cent mentioned that small family norms were also discussed. The study thus, indicates that only those local communities who participate in the health awareness programme are aware of the small family norms; as regards birth control methods a vast majority of 42.85 per cent reported that these were not discussed at all. With regard to alcoholism, a majority 45.71 per cent mentioned about alcoholism. Even, during investigation it was found that alcoholism is one of the major social problems in the village. But respondents regretted that no awareness campaign against alcoholism in the village was conducted so far. But over and above, the data reveals that programme on population related issues have played a greater role in generating awareness and motivation to parents and elders in the village. Regarding the family size, a majority 57.86 per cent are not aware what should be the size of the family. This level of awareness would also help to determine the attitude of the respondents towards the preference of the number of children. The data indicates only a small percentage of 14.99 per cent mentioned that small family norms means one to two children. With regard to the meaning of a small family, a majority 77.14 per cent stated that small family means better living conditions; again a majority of 60.71 per cent stated that good educational qualification is also another factor; and 59.28 per cent opined that small family also means better health conditions. Thus, the data show that majority of the respondents are aware that small family means a happy family. As regards the awareness about AIDS, not to speak of the causes, signs and symptoms of AIDS, 63.43 per cent respondents say that they had heard the term. With regard to the sources of information a majority, 34.28 per cent received knowledge and information from newspaper. Thus, the data indicates that neither communication media nor face-to-face communication alone can bring desired results on issues related to social life. Each media has different functions to perform in order to create awareness particularly for the local community in the rural areas.

Conclusion

An awareness programme can be organised as a part of population education after taking the whole community into confidence. Because, as individual of the deprived community they do not feel secure when dealt with an isolation from their communities. Thus, involvement of the community in the process of conscientisation brings into surface the feeling of discontent. This feeling may later lead to awareness and social action design to improve the quality of life of the people. General awareness programme conducted through population education in the community enables to understand the various factors influencing their lives. Population education can help in an overall socio-economic development with improvement in the quality of life. The satisfaction of their needs and aspiration of the community derive only when people are able to meet their basic needs, like food, energy, space, housing, health care, etc. Therefore, the learning plan for each community should be prepared according to the needs and demands of its specific situation and its particular stage of development. Below is given a broad outline of the topics of awareness programme:

- Learning-cum-discussion-group on problems of individual, family and the community.
- Causes of rapid population growth and the need for viable family size.
- Causes of poverty and the role of women in the management of resources.
- The need for literacy in the present day society.
- Issues related to the Government schemes for the upliftment of the poor.
- Health problem awareness including health of the mother and child and the ill effect of frequent pregnancies and prevention.

- Awareness about reproductive rights of women abortion, age of marriage and equality with men.
- Need of women to acquire skills in planning and decision making on population matters for their own family to prepare themselves as the change agents of the society.
- Infant mortality and awareness of causes of child illness.

All these awareness programmes could be provided as a part of population education which could be included in the curriculum of primary and secondary schools, and also at the college and university level.

NOTES

1. Moshini, S.R. (1993), *History of Adult Education in India,* New Delhi, pp. 183-184.
2. Kaur, Amrit, "Social and Economic Awareness as Components of Sustainable Development", *Indian Journal of Adult Education*, July-September, 1995, pp. 17-23.
3. Singh, U.K., Sudarsha, K.N. (1996), *Population Education*, New Delhi.
4. Yadav, S.R. (1999), *Adult Education Training and Productivity,* Indian Publication, Ambala Cant.

11

Awareness of Population Education Among the P.G. Students of North-Eastern Hill University, Shillong

Introduction

North-Eastern Hill University was set up by an Act of Parliament and notified on 19th July, 1973. The objects of the University as laid down in the Act, are to 'disseminate' an advance knowledge by providing instructional and research facilities in such branches of learning as it may deem fit; to pay special attention to the improvement of the social and economic conditions and welfare of the people of the hill areas of the North-Eastern Region, and in particular, their intellectual, academic and cultural advancement.

The jurisdiction of the university extended originally to the States of Meghalaya and Nagaland and the erstwhile Union Territories of Arunachal Pradesh and Mizoram. With the establishment of the Nagaland University on 6th September, 1994, the jurisdiction of NEHU over Nagaland ceased, and with the establishment of Mizoram University in June 2001, the jurisdiction of NEHU over Mizoram also ceased. However, the North-Eastern Regional Institute of Science and Technology located in Arunachal Pradesh is affiliated to NEHU.

Initially, the academic departments and the administration of NEHU at Shillong functioned from hired buildings. Meanwhile, the Government of Meghalaya acquired for the University a substantial plot of land (measuring about 1225 acres) a little outside the city limits for setting up its permanent campus. By 1991, the campus took the visible shape of a handsome university in the making. By 2004, nearly all the academic departments moved to new buildings on the permanent campus. The University now has Internet connectivity through own VSAT to which all the departments located in the campus are linked.

In spite of serious constraints of communication and the general lack of infrastructural facilities in the region, NEHU has established itself as an institution of learning and research of a very high quality. NEHU has been able to attract persons of proven academic excellence from almost all parts of the country to serve on its faculty; and its student community is drawn not only from different parts of North-East but also from other regions of the country. NEHU now has twenty-eight academic departments and five centres of studies under seven schools. Eight departments now received special grant from the University Grants Commission under SAP. In August 2005, the University is adding three new departments, namely Department of Statistics, Department of Law and the Department of Bio-Informatics and Bio-Technology.

Three Science departments also received grants under the UGC's COSIST programme. Some of the Departments have also received grants under the UGC's Department Research Support Scheme. In addition, the CSIR, DST, DAE UGC, Ford Foundation, DBT and DF & E have accorded a number of Research projects to individual members of the faculty. NEHU is a recipient of a number of endowments donated by various organisations and individuals including Dr. Shankar Dayal Sharma, former President of India and Justice Krishna Aier. NEHU was chosen for the prestigious Rajiv Gandhi chairs for research on protective discrimination and eastern para studies (Tribal Development). Several members of the faculty have been honoured with the highest academic awards in the country. Many teachers are involved in collaborative research projects with universities in Europe and Asia.

The University in order to fulfil its 'local' responsibility, as enshrined in its Act, focusing its attention on the North East in its curricular programme including research. At present there are fifty-seven undergraduate colleges affiliated to the University including eight professional colleges. The University Central Library has a holding of close to 2,40,000 books, 38,000 bound periodicals and it subscribes to 316 foreign and 366 Indian current journals. Recently, the facility of e-journals has been extended by the library for a number of internationally reputed journals belonging to various disciplines.

Of late there is an increasing number of in-campus recruitment. The number of students studying for their Master's degrees and research students working for their M.Phil. and Ph.D. degrees is close to 3000. The undergraduate colleges affiliated to the University enrol about 20,000 students. The University's faculty strength is just over 300.[1]

In a short span of about 33 years, NEHU has matured into an institution with a serious academic and social and cultural agenda for the future growth. Recently, NEHU has been chosen as a University with potential for excellence by the UGC.

The Centre for Adult and Continuing Education, one of the five centres of studies, is one of the oldest centres of the University which focuses its activities in teaching, research, extension and field outreach. There was a PERC functioning under the umbrella of CACE and carried out many field level programmes on Population Education, Adolescent Education, Women Empowerment, Gender Issues, Reproductive Health Care, HIV/AIDS and related issues. The CACE felt that it is desirable to carry out a study on the awareness of such issues among the P.G. students of NEHU and hence the study. The study was carried out with the following major objectives.

Objectives of the Study

1. To study the socio-economic status of the P.G. students of NEHU.
2. To study the awareness on women empowerment and issues related to women.
3. To study the awareness of HIV/AIDS.
4. To study all the areas related to sustainable development.

Methodology

A comprehensive questionnaire was developed by covering different areas related to the population and development education aiming at the sustainable development.

Sample

The study was carried out among the P.G. students of NEHU drawn from different schools of disciplines. The sample consists of 200 P.G. students who are undergoing M.A./M.Sc./M.Com./ M.Phil and Ph.D. programmes and P.G. Diploma in Adult and Continuing Education.

Sex

The following table illustrates sex-wise distribution of the respondents:

Table 11.1: Sex-wise Distribution of Respondents in Percentage

Sl. No.	*Sex*	*Percentage*
1.	Male	19.60
2.	Female	80.40
	Total	100.00

Among the total sample the female students (80.40%) out numbered the male (19.60%). Since the female population of the sample is very high the study itself will help to increase the quality of life of females which will ultimately reflect in their family life.

Religion

The following table indicates the distribution of the respondents according to their religion:

Table 11.2: Distribution of Respondents According to Religion in Percentage

Sl. No.	*Religion*	*Percentage*
1	Christians	86.00
2	Hindus	3.01
3	Unspecified	11.00
	Total	100.00

The Religion-wise analysis shows that there are Christians (86.60%), Hindus (3.01%) and the rest unspecified. The place of residence shows that there are students from urban (58.76%), Municipal area (12.37%) and rural (28.87%) as given in Table 11.3.

Migration

Table below shows the distribution of them according to their native areas:

Table 11.3: Distribution of Respondents According to the Native Areas

Sl. No.	*Religion*	*Percentage*
1	Urban	58.76
2	Municipal	12.37
3	Rural	28.87
	Total	100.00

Educational Level

The following table indicates the distribution of Parents Respondents according to qualification:

Table 11.4: Distribution of Parent Respondents According to Qualification in Percentage

Sl. No.	*Religion*	*Percentage*
1	Graduate	52.25
2	Undergraduates	41.75
3	Illiterate	8.00
	Total	100.00

Education of the Parents shows that 36 per cent of the Father and 16.05 per cent of Mother are graduates. It is to be noted that there are very few illiterate parents. All the parents are employed and mainly in the income group of Rs.7500 per month (45.36%). The analysis of number of children in the family shows that the birth control is not so common in Meghalaya.

Table 11.5: Number of Children in the Family in Percentage

1	2	3	4	5	6
28.87%	16.49%	15.46%	11.34%	11.34%	16.50%

The table (on page 157) shows the awareness of the P.G. students of NEHU on Women Empowerment and issues related to women, awareness on HIV/AIDS, population education and awareness on all the areas related to sustainable development.

Major Findings

Some of the major findings on the awareness of population education are given below:

(1) 56.70 per cent of the students are in favour to delay the birth of first child. 93.81 per cent are in favour that the girls should not marry till they attain puberty.

(2) Even though, the sample of female population is very high, they are of the opinion that women should not enjoy equal status with that of man (52.58%). But, they are of the opinion that female employment will negatively affect the family life (78.35%). Almost all are concerned about the increase of crime against women (95.88%).

(3) It is interesting to note that 36 per cent students favour the opinion that free availability of condoms will increase the sexual intercourse while 38.14 per cent not in favour of that. 78.35 per cent of the students are of the opinion that the visual media helped to increase

the criminal behaviour. Almost all students (97.93%) expressed the view that western cultures are influencing the nation.

Sl.No.	*Responses*	*Percentage*
1	To delay the birth of the first child	56.70
2	Girls should marry when they attain puberty	93.81
3	Women should not enjoy equal status with men	53.58
4	Female employment negatively affect family life	53.58
5	Increase of crime against women	78.35
6	Free availability of condoms—sexual intercourse	36.00
7	Not in favour of supply of free condoms	38.14
8	Visual media help to increase criminal behaviour	78.35
9	Western cultures influencing the nation	97.93
10	Alcohol is not good for health	92.78
11	Not using Drugs	50.00
12	Boys should marry at the age between 31-33	55.67
13	Boys should marry at the age between 28-30	38.14
14	Boys should marry at the age between 25-30	36.00
15	Girls should marry at the age between 18-20	37.11
16	Girls should marry at the age between 24-26	41.00
17	Girls should marry at the age between 27-30	22.00
18	Husband and wife are equally responsible for household works	88.60
19	Adolescent Education need to be introduced at high school level	87.63
20	STD/HIV/AIDS infection is very high among people who involve sexual intercourse with strangers	96.90
21	Awareness about World Population Day	16.49
22	International Women's Day	0.00
23	Current Indian Population	26.80
24	Frequent deliveries do not affect the health of women	52.47
25	Better communication between Husband and Wife	76.29
26	To have both sons and daughters in the family	56.70
27	Abortion is a crime	89.69
28	Prohibition of Alcohol in the State	50.00
29	Mental control is important to prevent AIDS infection	62.89
30	Women should be protected by men	50.51
31	Family welfare activities is necessary	100.00
32	Value based Education is important to prevent AIDS	100.00

(4) Similarly, the students have a clear awareness on the environmental problems, pollution, use of insecticides, etc.

(5) The students are fully aware that consumption of alcohol is not good for health (92.78%) and 50 per cent of the students are of the opinion that they are not using drugs.

(6) The awareness on the issues related to population explosion is moderate. It is important to note that 55.67 per cent students expressed the view that the boys should marry at the age between 31-33; 38.14 per cent between 28-30 and 36 per cent between 25-30 years of age. On the contrary, they are of the view that the girls should marry at the age between 18-20 (37.11%); 24-26 (41%) and only 22, per cent are in favour to marry at the age between 27-30 years. 88.6 per cent of the students are of the view that both husband and wife are equally responsible in household matters.

(7) It is important to note that 87.63% are of the opinion that adolescent education needs to be introduced at the high school level.

(8) The students are fully aware of the STD, AIDS infection, use of condoms, etc. They are of the opinion that STD/HIV/AIDS infection is very high among the persons who are involved in sexual intercourse with strangers (96.90%).

(9) The awareness about the World Population Day shows only 16.49 per cent and nobody is aware of the International Women's Day. Only 26.80 per cent is aware of the current Indian Population.

(10) It is interesting to note that frequent deliveries do not affect the health of women is favoured by 82.47 per cent. Among the sample 76.29 per cent favour that there should be better communication between husband and wife.

(11) 56.70 per cent students are in favour that there must be a son even if the first two children are daughter which still shows the male pre-dominancy in the society.

(12) 89.69 per cent are in favour of abortion.

(13) 50 per cent of the students are in favour of imposing total prohibition of alcohol in the State.

(14) 62.89 per cent for the students are of the opinion that mental control is more important than physical control to prevent AIDS infection.

(15) 50.51 per cent of the students are of the opinion that women should be protected by men.

(16) All students unanimously expressed the view that the family welfare activities should be never ending process.

(17) All students are of the view that value based education should be strengthened to control AIDS.

The study revealed the fact the the P.G. students of the NEHU has comparatively good awareness on the various aspects of population education, sustainable development, awareness on social issues, poverty, unemployment, quality of life, women empowerment, gender issues, reproductive health care, population control, substance abuse, HIV/AIDS, STD, environmental population, value education, etc.

REFERENCE

1. North-Eastern Hill University Prospectus 2005-06, pp.1-4.

17. See "Laban Dorbar Expresses Concern Over Pollution Rise", *Meghalaya Guardian*, Vol. IX, No. 151, dated June 5, 1998, p. 1.
18. See "Cleaning Drive", *Meghalaya Guardian*, dated March 26, 1998, p.1.
19. See "Public Hearing on Environment and Development", *Meghalaya Guardian*, dated July 3, 1998, p.1.
20. Mazhari, H.K., "Community Based Solid Waste Management—Lummawrie Experience", a Seminar Paper presented on "Environmental Hygiene" organised by the NEICSSR, Shillong, at Don Bosco Youth Centre, Shillong, dated June 5, 1996, pp. 2-3.
21. *Ibid.*, p. 56.
22. For details see *Report of an Awareness Campaign on "Women's Role on Waste Utilisation-cum-Exhibition"*, organised by Ka Lympung Ki Seng Kynthei, Shillong on May 13, 1995 at Laban, Shillong, pp. 1-11.

12

Population Explosion in India

The fast increasing population of the world constitutes a danger signal to humanity. Every country in the world is concerned about the unprecedented explosion in human numbers. The greatest problem facing our country today is the unbridled growth of population. According to a new World Bank report, the study shows that India which is now the second most populous country in the world after China with 934 million people will grow to 1.4 billion by the year 2030. China with 1.2 billion will remain the population giant with 1.5 billion in 2030. Whereas United States will remain the third most populous country with 298 million from 263 million in 1995, and Indonesia will be the fourth country with 274.7 million by increasing 192.5 million.[1] From 1995 to 2030 world population will grow slightly less than 50 per cent, but the growth rates by continent vary widely. Africa's population will grow to 116 per cent, from 720 million in 1995 to 1.6 billion in 35 years and Asia's countries will grow to 47 per cent, from 3.4 billion to 5.1 billion in 35 years.[2] The World Bank Population Projection 1994-95 report says during the next 35 years, global population will increase to around 8.5 billion, with almost 90 per cent of the increase occurring in developing countries. About 70 per cent of the increase will occur in the very poorest developing countries.[3]

In South Asia, Afghanistan will record the highest increase at 146.3 per cent (from 23 million to 57 million), followed by Maldives with 128.3 per cent (251,000 to 128,000),Bhutan 101.2 per cent (16 million to 32 million), Pakistan 99.7 per cent (129 million to 259 million) and Nepal

90 per cent (21 million to 40 million), Sri Lanka will have the slowest increase in population from 18 million to 24 million (an increase of 35 per cent), India will increase to 53.3 per cent and Bangladesh from 121 million to 191 million (an increase of 57 per cent).[4]

The Disaster within 35 years is that:

- World population would grow by 50 per cent to 100 per cent.
- Twenty-five developing countries, including the entire Near East and North Africa except Turkey, would have insufficient water for their people.
- World energy consumption would increase by 35 per cent.
- Thinning of the ozone layer surrounding earth would reduce crop yields and fish catches and caused increased rates of skin cancer and blindness.
- Global warming could cause sea levels to rise, flooding coastal areas.[5]

Population Increase in India

Although the fastest population growth rates are found in Africa, more than half of all global population occurs in Asia, with an annual population increase of over 57 million. The World Development report project that in the year 2020, there will be an estimated one billion Indians, fighting of shelter, employment, food, wealth and also for socio-political power.[6] Unchecked population growth poses the most serious threat to life on planet earth. As per the 1991 census, India accounts for 16 per cent of the world population, as compared to about 15 per cent in the last decade. The countries with dense population are China with 21.7 per cent, USSR 6.0 per cent and USA. 5.0 per cent. India alone with these three countries (China, USSR and USA.) accounts for nearly half (48.3%) of the world population.

The total population of India in 1600 was estimated to be 10.0 crores. However, it increases to 25.4 crores in 1871 and further increase to 27.89 crore in 1931. In 1941 the population of India raised to 31.86 crore and goes up to 36.10 crore in 1951. It further increases to 43.92 crore in 1961; 54.81 crore in 1971 and 68.51 crore in 1981. The total population of India as on March 1, 2001 stood at 1027 million people with 5312 million males and 4957 million females. Thus, India added 39.69 million people to the population during 1931-41. In 1941-51 it added 42.42 million; in 1951-61 it added 108.92 million; in 1961-71 to 137.02 million; and raise to 158.74 million in 1981-91. The net increase of population during the three decades from 1931-61 it was 161 million and from 1961-91 it went up to 404 million. The percentage of increase between 1921-51 to 1961-91 was 12.9 and 98.4 per cent, respectively. The addition of 158.74 million people in 1981-91 means an addition of 158.74 lakh persons every year; 13.22 lakh every month; 44.09 thousand persons everyday, or about 1837 persons every hour, and 31 persons every minute.[7] In comparison to this, the increase in number of persons per minute was 21 in 1961-71; 15 in 1951-61 and eight in 1941-51. This increase in number of persons shows that the rate of growth of population during the decades of the present century as compared by now is faster as well as alarming.

Disaster is that:

- Every sixth person in the world today is an Indian. By the turn of the century, every fifth living person will be an Indian.
- India adds about 10 lakh persons to its population every three weeks.
- Every year, at the growth rate of 21.38 (2001 census), India was adding one Australia to its population and that if the growth rate remain constant, the increase in absolute terms would expand every year especially as the life expectancy has steadily risen now to 60 years.
- India alone adds nearly as many people each year to the population of the world as all of Sub-Saharan Africa.
- By the turn of the twenty-first century, India would overtake China as the world's most populous nation,

with India's population reaching 1642.8 million as compared with China's 1,530 million.

- More than three times as many couples enter the reproductive span than those living it, with the fertility rate of the younger group three times higher than that of those passing out of the reproductive range.
- If current trends in population and economic growth continue and no further measures are taken to protect the environment and conserve resources, the planet and its people would face serious consequences. For example, life for most people would be unbearable, medical facilities would be difficult to provide, expenses on education, housing, etc. would be exorbitant and scarcity of food would plunge three-fifth of the nations below the poverty line.

If No change

If trends do not change, population experts predict that in just five years, by the end of the decade:[9]

- The world would have one billion more people than it had in 1990.
- More than half of the developing countries would be unable to feed their people without importing food.
- One-fourth of the world's fresh water supply would be too polluted to drink.
- Most tropical forests would be severely damaged or destroyed; large tropical forests might remain in only a handful of countries.
- Thousands of plant and animal species would disappear before scientists had an opportunity to assess their usefulness to humankind.

Causes of Population Growth

Causes of population explosion in India may be classified as follows:

(i) Widening Gap between Birth and Death Rates

The average annual birth rate in India has declined right from the decade 1931-41. The birth rate has declined from 45 per thousand during 1931-41 to 43 per thousand in 1941-51. Then it slightly comes down to 44 per thousand during the decade 1951-61. In 1980 the birth rate showed a further decline. It was 33.7 per thousand in comparison to 37 per thousand in 1971-81. In 1989, the birth rate further declined to 30.5 per thousand in comparison to 31.5 per thousand in 1988 and 23.0 in 2001. On the other hand, the death rate has also shown a similar decline from 33 per thousand during 1931-41 to 31 per thousand in 1941-51. It comes down to 26 per thousand during the decade 1951-61. In 1980, the death rate showed a further decline. It was 12.6 per thousand in comparison to 15.0 per thousand in 1971-81. In 1989, the death rate was 10.2 per thousand per year in comparison to 11.0 in 1988[10] and to 9.7 in 2001. Since birth rate has shown a marginal decline and death rate has come down rather sharply, the widening gap has increased India's population rapidly.

(ii) Low Age at Marriage

Child marriages have been very common in India. Of the four million marriages which takes place in India in a year, three million are of girls who are under the legal age of 18. However, the International Planned Parenthood Federation was alarmed at this age as in adolescent young girls are not emotionally or physically ready for child bearing. Even today, it was found that 18 per cent of girls in Asia, 16 per cent in Africa and 8 per cent in Latin America are married by the age of 15. As a result, child birth leads to higher rates of maternal mortality and morbidity. Pregnancy related deaths are the main cause of 15-19 year old woman all over the world.[11]

According to the 1951 Census, in India it was found that 72.0 per cent marriages were performed before 15 years of age and 34 per cent before ten years of age. This resulted in a continuous increase in the mean age at marriage among males and females. The mean age at marriage of females has increased from 13.1 in 1901 to 13.2 in 1911 and raised from 12.7 in 1921 to 13.7 in 1931, 14.7 in 1941, 15.6 in 1951, 16.1 in 1961, 17.2 in 1971, 17.6 in 1981 to 18 years in 1991. Against this, the mean age at marriage of males has considerably increased from 20.0 in 1901 to 20.7 in 1921 and further raised to 19.2 in 1951 to 21.4 in 1961, 22.2 in 1971 and 22.6 in 1981.[12] Though, the mean age at marriage had been continuously increasing, yet a large number of girls even today marry at an age at which they are not ready for marriage either socially and emotionally.

Age of women at marriage is also closely related to the infant mortality rate. In India 57.1 per cent of women under 20 years are married. While the average number of children per married women in India was 4.5, it was only 3.6 in Sri Lanka and 2.5 in China. Of the 25 million children born every year in India, two million children die before reaching the age of one year. According to the UNICEF study, it was mentioned that majority of these deaths were due to avoidable infections and malnutrition. As per the latest estimates India place Infant Mortality Rate (IMR) at 79 and the under-five mortality rate at 124 per 1000 live births. The study also mentioned that 90 of the 145 countries surveyed had lowered infant mortality rate than India, and 103 nations lowered under-five mortality rate. These included developing nations like Botswana, Kenya, Zimbabwe, Egypt, Morocco, Sri Lanka, Vietnam and all countries in Central and South America. In India IMR ranged from 17 per 1000 live births in Kerala to 114 in Orissa. In rural areas IMR exceeded the IMR in urban areas and the gap continued to persist. In 1990, IMR in rural areas of 86 per 1000 live births was higher than the IMR in urban areas twenty years ago (82 per thousand births in 1971). In India, the current IMR level in urban areas as a whole, was estimated at 51 per 1000 live births. About 38.8 million people live below the poverty line in urban areas and that 15 to 16 million children do not have adequate basic health care, nutrition, safe drinking water and education.[13]

As per the Extensive Surveys by the National Institute of Nutrition, the study focus that in India out of 77 million children aged 1 to 5 years nearly 48 per cent suffered malnutrition; of the 60 per cent families studied one family lost one or more children under the age of five, and 35 per cent had lost one to three children. Only 15 per cent of the families had escaped child death. While the national averages in infant mortality have come down to 96 per 1000 live births in Kerala it was 42 while in U.P. it was 115 to 178 live births in spite of the fact that income-wise and nutrition-wise the conditions are not dissimilar. The main problems of infant mortality were due to lack of cleanliness, balanced diet, health education especially of mothers, ante-natal care, skilled care at delivery and general ignorance. Most of the Indian women are exposed to pregnancy almost from puberty onwards for a much longer number of years.[14] Thus, malnutrition, high levels of infection, lack of basic facilities and ignorance are the factors which lead not only to women who are physically weak, but also to children who are born with a poor physical and mental heritage.

(iii) High Illiteracy

Illiteracy has been one of the key factors in the population explosion. According to the 2001 census, the number of illiterates above the age of seven plus was 300.14 million against 328.88 number of literate persons in the last decade. Although the percentage of literacy in the country was 65.38 per cent, the number of illiterates had surpassed the literates. According to Prof. Weiner, India was the single largest producers of world's illiterates. While the literacy rate improved in each decade since Independence, the absolute number of illiterates in the country has risen from 294 million in 1951[15] to 482 million in 1991 and came down to 300.14 million by 2001. Prof. Weiner, further pointed out that as many India's literacy rate of 36 per cent, many of the neighbouring countries in Asia have crossed the 70 per cent rate. For instance, it was 85.0 per cent in China, 95.6 per cent in Thailand, 97.8 per cent in South Korea, 95 per cent in North Korea, 88 per cent in Sri Lanka, 95.4 in Philippine, 93.3 in Vietnam, 87.5 in Malaysia and 84.7 in Myanmar.[16] Weiner, further pointed out that in many poor countries in Africa, including Botswana, Swaziland, Lesoto, Zimbabwe, Madagascar, Zambia, Ghana, Tanzania, Zaire and South Africa the literacy rate was substantially higher than

India. In these countries, the rate of primary school attendance was well ahead than India.[17]

(iv) Women's Education

Education of women is another factor that is hindered by population increase. Women who have neither functional nor formal education will continue to be looked into stereotyped roles of dependence and regarded them as liability rather than as an asset in socio-economic development. Women's age at marriage of the first born child and decision-making powers on family size depend largely on their educational endowment. Improvement in female literacy has a direct effect on reducing fertility. In most of the districts of major states in India it was found where a high proportion of women could read and write the average number of children per woman was considerably lower than in districts where literacy levels were low. Also, in high literacy districts, a greater proportion of children survived infancy. Lower child mortality contributed lower fertility rates. Higher female literacy resulted in lower fertility. One of the main reasons why Kerala leads in low birth and death rates is because of the high level of literacy among women. Despite improvements in female literacy levels in India as a whole, only about one in four Indian women is literate.[18] The findings of the 1991 Census shows that women in India lack in literacy. While 63.86 per cent of Indian men are literate, only 39.5 per cent of women in India can read and write. This low level of literacy has been the primary cause of contributing to nearly half the population growth in the country. Female literacy rates in India vary from region to region. While 87 per cent of the women in the uppermost State of Kerala are literate, only 21 per cent of women in northern State of Rajasthan can claim to be literate. States with high female literacy rates usually have low rates of population growth. In Kerala where female literacy is the highest in India, its annual population growth rate reduces to 1.3 per cent by 1991. With every increase in the Indian population, the numbers of illiterate women also increase. In 1981, there were 181 million illiterate women in India and increase to 199 million in 1991. This shows an increase of 16 million in one decade. But with every decade the percentage of literate women in India is also increasing from 9 per cent in 1951 to 15.35 per cent in 1961; 22 per cent in 1971; 30 per cent in 1981; 39.29 per cent in 1991 and 54.16 in 2001. Female literacy was finally emerging as a priority for the Government of India to set up the National Literacy Mission in 70 districts of the country in 1988.[19] The mission which works through voluntary agencies tried to educate under-privileged groups, including women. As a result, some success had already been noted. This is evident from the fact that in 1991 Kerala was declared fully-literate with 90.59 per cent overall literacy rates (74.8 per cent female literacy rate). Other southern districts also experiencing the effects of female literacy like demand for equal wages, an anti-liquor agitation and improvement of child health etc. Thus, education has quietly changing the lives of these women at least.

(v) Socio-Cultural and Religious Attitude Towards Family Planning

Rooted customs, traditions and socio-cultural beliefs in favour of large families continue to be the greatest impediments in achieving family planning. Moreover, religious factors also hinder the implementation of family planning. There are women who did not agree family planning on the plea that they cannot go against the wishes of God. There are some who agree that the purpose of a woman's life is to bear children. On the other hand, malnutrition, high levels of infection, lack of basic facilities and ignorance are the factors which are compounded by almost in human social attitudes and prejudices which pervade tradition-bound societies and lead not only to women who are physically weak, but to children who are born with a poor physical and mental heritage, thus effecting the nation at large. Despite more than forty years of planning, the problem of population explosion in India still defies a solution. The continuing rapid growth in population over these years undermined the country's planning process. The Ministry of Health and Family Welfare at the Centre, however, identified the population explosion as the most pressing problem facing the country. The experience in the conduct of family planning programme over the years had brought about the importance of taking a holistic approach towards the problem of population control. Social factors such as female literacy, age at marriage of girls, status of women and position of women's employment play a vital role in determining the success of the progamme. It was through these factors that the programme was implemented as Family Welfare programme with mother and child care as its integral part.

Other Causes

Some of the other causes responsible for the increase in population are joint family system and lack of responsibility of young couples in families to bring up their children, lack of recreational facilities and lack of awareness about the adverse effects of population explosion.

Many poor women produce children not because they are ignorant but because they need them. This is evident from the fact that there are 35 million child workers in India. As per the 1981 Census, the child labour in India between the age-group 0-14 years was 11,168. Out of which agricultural labourers accounted for 42.75 per cent of the total, and another 35.93 per cent are cultivators.[20] According to Joseph Gathia, Director of the Centre of Concern for Child Labour, pointed out that the main cause that makes children drop-out of school and seek employment was not because of poverty but lack of sound educational infrastructure. In such cases, he highlighted that field experience had shown that parents were eager to send their children to school but in the absence of proper educational facilities the parents felt that children could better utilize their time in wage employment than education.[21] Child labour is closely related to the rate of school drop-outs. As per the figures available at the Labour Ministry, Government of India, drop-outs are the highest in Bihar and Andhra Pradesh with 80.53 per cent and 74.18 per cent respectively. While the lowest drop-out rate occurs in Kerala with only 15.92 per cent. The reason that led Kerala's low drop-out rate was the existence of a good supportive system of education. Even poor people in Kerala send their children to school at least up to the primary level. Whereas, in other States like Bihar and Uttar Pradesh, people placed in similar economic circumstances.[22]

Effects of Population Explosion

Population growth has a direct effect on the standards of living and style of life. The effects of population growth are manifold in terms of retarding development and causing destructive pressures on the environment. The appalling over-crowding of cities and towns has brought about a virtual break-down of transportation, electricity and other services. Over-population also led to the rise of crime and an increase in conflict in the urban and semi-urban areas. If the population continues to increase by 16 million every year, in a few years from now India will suffer from people who will fight against employment, food, shelter and clothing. As of now, even for the present population of 1027 million (2001 Census), it is futile to think of jobs for all, shelter for all, education for all or health for all by 2000 A.D.

It has been calculated that for every addition of about 135 million people in India, the people will require 1.35 lakh primary and middle schools, 10 thousand higher secondary schools, 50 lakh primary and middle school teachers, 1.5 lakh higher secondary school teachers, 4000 hospitals and dispensaries, 1500 primary health centres, two lakh hospital beds, 50 thousand doctors, 25 thousand nurses, 20 million tonnes cereals, 25,000 metres of cloth and 2,500 million houses.[23] If India do not take up the issue of controlling population explosion seriously, the future of the country is very doomed.

Conclusion

India uses a system of Five-Year Plans to achieve higher standards of living and better opportunities for its people. With the rapid increase in population without a corresponding increase in resources per capita, living standards are naturally low. There has not been an effective institutionalized mechanism to reduce birth rate. Moreover, efforts to bring down the death rate have been quire successful. A high rate of population growth is bound to adversely affect the economic progress of the country. Today, policies of economic development have not been very effective because the increase in production is absorbed by the growth of population. Therefore, it is important that government and voluntary agencies take effective measures to check population growth. At the same time, measures to raise the mean age of marriage, female literacy and education, mother and child survival, health poverty alleviation and expanding economic opportunities including skills-training for income generation are the key elements in checking population growth. As to the family planning programme itself, there are seven major factors that must be tackled successfully. These are: (i) a strong political will exerted from the highest levels all the way down to the village panchayat; (ii) a flexible and responsive administration; (iii) active participation by several concerned Ministries and Departments in addition to the Ministry of Health and Family Welfare; (iv) integrating or interlinking family planning with other allied measures; (v) effective information, education and motivation campaigns to different sectors of the people concerned; (vi) providing quality services and diversifying them to reach the doorsteps of the people, with an adequate follow-up and providing a choice of method. Lastly, evoking community participation so that people themselves became the promoters as well as the users of family planning methods to achieve the small family norm.[24]

The following suggestions may be put forward to control population explosion:

(1) Group acceptance of the small size family.
(2) Personal knowledge about family planning methods.
(3) Ready availability of birth-control devices and services.
(4) Controlling early marriages.

NOTES

1. See "India Second Most Populous Country", *Shillong Times* (Shillong), Vol. XLIX, No. 348 dated August 8, 1994, p. 4.
2. *Ibid.*
3. *Ibid.*
4. *Ibid.*
5. Population Reports, May 1992.
6. See "Population Explosion: The Real Problem", *Meghalaya Guardian* (Guwahati), Vol. III, No. 46, dated February 18, 1992, p. 4.
7. "*Occasional Monograph on World Population Growth*", published by Indian Institute of Ecology and Environment, New Delhi.
8. United Nations, "Determinants and Consequences of Population Trends", Vol. I (New York, 1973).
9. Population Report, May 1992.
10. *Occasional Monograph on World Population Growth*, published by Indian Institute of Ecology and Environment,.New Delhi.
11. See "Three Million Girls Marry Before 18 in India:, *Meghalaya Guardian* (Guwahati), dated May 31, 1994, p. 2.
12. Handbook on Social Welfare Statistics, 1981, p. 50.
13. See "India Leading in Infant Mortality Rate per 1000", *Meghalaya Guardian* (Guwahati), Vol.V, No. 256 dated September 19, 1994, p. 3.
14. Wadia, A.B., "*The Empowerment of Women: Population and Development*" published by the Family Planning Association of India, (FPAI), (Bombay, 1992), p. 6.
15. See "Compulsory Education Can End Child Labour", *Meghalaya Guardian* (Guwahati), Vol.V, No.II dated January 11, 1994, p. 3.
16. *UNESCO 1999 Statistical Year Book* (Estimated Literacy Rates for the Year 2000).
17. F.N. 15.
18. *Asia-Pacific Population and Policy*, No. 15, dated December 1990, p. 12.
19. *People and the Planet*, Vol.II, No. 1, 1993, p. 10.
20. See "Child Labour", *Meghalaya Guardian* (Guwahati), Vol.V, No. 261, dated September 24, 1994, p. 5.
21. See "Lack of Sound Educational Infrastructure Responsibility", *Meghalaya Guardian* (Guwahati), Vol.V, No. 258, dated September 20, 1994, p. 3.
22. *Ibid.*
23. *India Today* (New Delhi), dated September 16-30, 1979, p. 53.
24. Wadia, A.B., "Population Growth", published by Family Planning Association of India, New Delhi, 1992, p. 5.

SECTION IV

Extension Education: Impact on Literacy Skills

13

Need to Introduce Life Skills Education to Child Labourers: Shillong Experience

Introduction

Child labour refers to the employment of children in gainful occupations or a material contribution to the income of the family. It is both economic and social evil. Thus, this leads to serious health hazards and denies them opportunity for physical and mental health. The children are our nation's resource. The children involved in child labour cannot be neglected. They also need appropriate Life Skills Education Programmes at their own level in Non-Formal way.

The problem of child labour is a world phenomenon. About 210.8 million children in the age-group of 5-14 years of age are engaged in some form of economic activity. Of these 186.3 million fall within the strict definition of child labour. Most of these child labours are concentrated in the developing countries.[1] In developed countries children work for their pocket money. Whereas, in developing countries they work for the economic need. In underdeveloped countries they mainly work for their parents, family and for themselves.

In India, children constitutes 36 per cent of India's population and a bulk of them still suffer from malnutrition, poverty, disease, exploitation and on top of all, illiteracy[2]. In other sense India's more than 50 per cent children are deprived of all amenities and facilities enjoyed by the other half. India has the largest number of child labours in the world. One-third of these children under the age of 16 years are forced to work, often in the most dreadful conditions and work for long hours. Further, there are about 74 million children who are neither enrolled in schools nor accounted for in the labour forced. These came under the category of "Nowhere Child"[3]. It is the need of the hour to focus on this sector of the community and provide Life Skills Education for increasing the quality of life.

The incidence of child labour in India is more rural than urban. The National Commission on labour points out that more than 90.87 per cent of the working children are in the rural areas and employed in agricultural and allied activities. In the urban unorganized sector child labour are employed in small-scale cottage industries, restaurants, workshops, domestic service and on streets. About two million children are engaged in employment which is characterised as hazardous[4]. Even though statistics are available with the Government, suitable steps have not been taken to focus in imparting Life Skills Education programmes to them.

Looking at the size of the problem, a number of reasons forces parents to send their children to work as child labourers. The main reason is poverty which forces them to push their children to contribute to the family income. Secondly, poor families are not educated enough to understand the implications of sending their children to work. These parents wish their children to work to keep them occupied and off the streets so that they do not get into the mischief. Children also work when they do no perform well in school and have no other alternative. In some instances, home situation compels children to work and earn independently. When a family migrates from rural to urban areas they face the unknown labour situation which brings them instability and insecurity for the family which compels the children to work for the survival of the family[5]. The NGOs/Government agencies/ University CACEES/National Service Scheme/Social Welfare Department etc. need to make combined effort to develop appropriate Life Skills Education and Youth Development Programmes for the overall development of these children both formally and non-formally.

The International Labour Organisation (ILO) has also stressed the problems raised by the existence of child labour. In 1979, a resolution was adopted by the ILO calling for social and legislative action for the elimination of child labour. Various international agencies concerned with the welfare of children have been asking India to eliminate child labour. Over the years, India has taken several steps to tackle the problem[6]. Article 24 of the Constitution of India states that no child below the age of 14 years should be employed to work in any factory or mine or engaged in any hazardous employment. Chapter IV of the Constitution of India contains specific directions in relation to welfare of children. Article 39 states that "the State shall, in particular, direct its policy towards securing ... (a) that the health and strength of workers, women and men and the tender age of children are not abused and their citizens are not forced by economic necessity to enter avocations unsuited to their age of children; and (b) that children and youth are protected against exploitation and against moral and material abandonment. Even though such legislations are there in reality it is not possible to wipe out the child labour problem totally because the Government has no other alternatives for rehabilitation or any other effective mechanism to meet the need of this deprived section of the community. The only way is to provide appropriate Life Skills which will help attitudinal changes among them which may ultimately lead to their overall development.

Besides constitutional provisions, the Government of India also regulates the employment of children through many legislative measures like Employment of Children Act, 1935; Employment of Children (Prohibition and Regulation) Act, 1986; Factories Act, 1948; Mines Act, 1952; Plantation Labour Act, Motor Vehicle Act, 1951 and Shops and Commercial Establishment Acts of various States.

In spite of the above statutory measures children are more engaged in different activities. Employers engaged more children to reduce the production cost and increase profit, engaging them for more hours without facing any protest from them.

Significance of the Study

In order to study the details of the problems of the child labourers, it was decided to carry out a study in Shillong, the capital of Meghalaya, in the north-eastern region of the country. In Shillong city, child labour exists in tea-stalls, hotels, restaurants, motor-garages, quarries, agriculture, streets trading and among domestic servants. It is very much interesting to study the socio-economic conditions, working conditions, hazards involve in the jobs in which they are engaged and their consciousness towards legislation and own future as well as the effectiveness of our legislative procedures and machineries to prohibit and regulate the prevailing system in the city, types of life skills they possess etc.

Objectives of the Study

The following are the objectives of the study:

(1) To study the socio-economic conditions of the child labour in Shillong city.
(2) To identify the factors which compels them to accept employment from childhood.
(3) To analyze the type of jobs they are doing.
(4) To observe the consciousness towards legislation and their own future plan.
(5) To identify the life skills they possess.

Materials and Methods

A comprehensive questionnaire was developed by covering different areas relating to child labour. Primary data was collected by using a structural interview schedule and personal observation for the concerned children. Investigation was carried out covers the whole areas of the greater Shillong area. Altogether, twenty-three (23) localities under the greater Shillong area and the suburb areas of Shillong city are investigated for the study. *Ïewduh* (Bara Bazar), and *Khyndailad* (Police Bazar), a majority of these child labourers where concentration is more are found working in commercial areas like *Ïewduh* and *Khyndailad*. The work of these child labourers constitute mostly of rag picking, cleaning automobiles, selling betel nut, posters, shoe polishing, tea boy, domestic help and others. The sample is conducted selecting 100 child labour on the basis of random sampling method. Secondary data is used by consulting books, journals, magazines, newspapers, etc.

Demographic Features of Sample Respondents

Table 13.1: Sex-wise Distribution of Sample Respondents

Sl. No.	*Sex*	*Total*	*Percentage*
1	Male	80	80
2	Female	20	20
	Total	**100**	**100**

Among the total sample the male respondents (80%) outnumbered the female (20%) showing the dominance of male population in the sample. Because male children are stronger and more exposed to dangers of streets and work places they are preferred to girls.

Table 13.2: Distribution of Sample Respondents According to Age

Sl. No.	*Age-Group*	*Total*	*Percentage*
1	Below 8 years	6	6.00
2	8-12 years	46	46.00
3	12-14 years	48	48.00
	Total	**100**	**100.00**

Majority 48 per cent of these child labourers is found in the age-group of 12-14 years and are in engaged in different sectors. 46 per cent are found in the age-group of 8-12 years and only 6 per cent are below 8 year of age. It is found from the study that most of them 70 per cent have entered into work at the age of nine. Most of them are engaged in servicing work like washing motor-bikes, scooters, cars, etc., some are doing mechanic work like welding work in the workshop and others are engaged in burning the charcoal. Children below eight years of age are found in street trading like selling posters, selling pan, *biri*, cigarette, newspapers and chemical items like computer, TV and window glass and tape recorder cleaning. Some are helping their mothers at beetle shops.

Under the Child Labour (Prohibition and Regulation) Act of 1986, 'child' means a person who has not completed his fourteenth year of age and 'adolescent' means a person who has completed his fourteenth and has not completed his eighteenth years of age. According to this definition, children constitutes 54.28 per cent of the total sample whereas adolescent constitutes only 4.72 per cent of the total sample respondents.

Table 13.3: Distribution of Respondents According to Religion

Sl. No.	*Religion*	*Total*	*Percentage*
1	Christian	60	60.00
2	Hindu	18	18.00
3	Muslims	6	6.00
4	Indigenous	8	8.00
5	Others	8	8.00
	Total	**100**	**100.00**

Table above reveals that Christians are in majority, followed by Hindu 18 per cent and Muslim 6 per cent. The indigenous constitute 8 per cent and other religions like Sikh, etc. constitute another 8 per cent of the total sample respondent.

Migration

Almost all the respondents are migrated from different areas to the capital town either with their parents, relatives or employers. Table 13.4 shows the distribution of the respondents according to their native areas.

Out of the total respondents 84 per cent are migrated from the rural areas to the town from outside the district. While 10 per cent have migrated from their native place to the semi-urban areas of Shillong city and 6 per cent are migrated to urban areas within the district to get employment. The main cause of migration is no doubt poverty and unavailability of earning resources at the native places.

Table 13.4: Distribution of Respondents According to their Native Area

Sl. No.	*Area*	*Total*	*Percentage*
1	Urban	6	6.00
2	Semi-Urban	10	10.00
3	Rural	84	84.00
	Total	**100**	**100.00**

Family Size

As family size and ratio of earners and dependents influences the child employment, it is essential to know the family background.

Table 13.5: Distribution of Sample Respondents According to Family Size

Sl. No.	*Size of the Family*	*Total*	*Percentage*
1	Below 5	24	24.00
2	5-8 years	62	62.00
3	8 and above	14	14.00
	Total	**100**	**100.00**

The table above shows that only 14 per cent of the respondents are from the families having eight or more members. It is also found that 24 per cent are from the families having below five members. A large majority of the respondents 62 per cent shows that they are from the families having five to eight members. Commonly these respondents doing labour work are from the poor with big families. Although earners per family increase with family size, the dependents increase at a higher rate than earners. As such, it becomes difficult for the earner to provide proper fooding, clothing, etc. to all the members. As a result it compels very eligible members to work and earn for the family. Thus, either parents send their children to work or the respondents voluntarily accept work for supplementing their family income.

Educational Background

In spite of government efforts to increase the literacy rate illiteracy is still increasing. Illiteracy leaves no way for children but to accept employment from childhood. Table below shows the educational background of respondents.

Table 13.6: Distribution of Respondents According to Education

Sl. No.	*Educational Level*	*Total*	*Percentage*
1	Illiterate	36	36.00
2	Upto Class III	26	26.00
3	Class IV to Class VII	8	8.00
4	Class VIII and above	4	4.00
5	Attending schools with work	26	26.00
	Total	**100**	**100.00**

The above table shows that 74 per cent of children have drop-out from schools. Out of which 36 per cent are illiterate and have not attending schools before. Thus, the table reveals that a large number of child labourers are illiterate. Another 26 per cent reach up to the primary level or below. Only 8 per cent reach up to Class IV or below Class VII. A small percentage of 4 per cent are educated up to Class VIII and above. Interestingly, 26 per cent are found working and attending morning schools.

To know the reason why these sample respondents leave education, the table 13.7 will show the reasons why they left education from such an early age.

74 per cent of the respondents reported that they could not attend schools or drop-out from schools because of poverty. Out of which, 4 per cent mentioned that their parents were not interested for their study. While another 12 per cent stated that they left schooling as they had no interest. Another 34

per cent mentioned that they have to share their family burden and thus compelled them to leave education and accept work. Since majority of the parents of these respondents are illiterate they have no interest in sending their children to school but feel that earning something is more important for the family than to read and write.

Table 13.7: Distribution of Respondents According to Cause of Leaving Education

Sl. No.	*Cause*	*Total*	*Percentage*
1	Poverty	24	24.00
2	Parents not interested	4	4.00
3	Child not interested	12	12.00
4	Other reasons	34	34.00
	Total	**100**	**100.00**

Present Living

It is important to know whether these children respondents are residing with their parents or not. The following table shows thc present living conditions of these children.

Table 13.8: Distribution of Sample Respondents According to their Present Living

Sl. No.	*Residence*	*Total*	*Percentage*
1	Living with parents	90	90.00
2	Living with relatives	2	2.00
3	Living independently but have relations with family	4	4.00
4	Living independently but no relation with family	4	4.00
	Total	**100**	**100.00**

The above table shows that a large percentage 90 per cent of the children respondents are living with their parents in different localities of the greater Shillong city. Two per cent stay with their relatives in Shillong city. Another four per cent of these respondents are living independently which are mostly at the work place inside hotels, verandas of shops, etc. even though they have relationship with their families may be in Shillong or at their village. Another four per cent mentioned of having no relationship with their families as they left home and live independently.

Table 13.9: Occupation-wise Distribution of Sample Respondents

Sl. No.	*Occupation*	*Total*	*Percentage*
1	Work in Hotel/Restaurant	18	18.00
2	Garage and Motor Servicing work	14	14.00
3	Welding works	2	2.00
4	Betel shops	4	4.00
5	Tailoring work	0	0.00
6	Household work	12	12.00
7	Mason work	4	4.00
8	Carpentry work	0	0.00
9	Self-Employment like collecting tin, polythenes, etc.	14	14.00
10	Street trading	32	32.00
	Total	**100**	**100.00**

Out of the total sample respondents (100%), 18 per cent are employed in different hotel and restaurants which are the easiest available job and needs no education and experience. 14 per cent of them are engaged in garage and motor servicing works. They work as trainee mechanic and helper in welding and washing the car, motor-bike, scooter, etc. Another two per cent are engaged in welding works, four per cent are helping their mothers in small betel shops, to support the need of the family. 12 per cent of the respondents are employed as domestic servants to do the household works to wash utensils, clean the rooms, wash the clothes, care for the baby at home, etc. Four per cent are engaged in mason works at various places either with their family or independently. Fourteen per cent from among the respondents have engaged themselves for collecting broken tin, iron, glasses, polythenes, etc. from the road-sides of the Shillong city. While a large majority, 32 per cent are in the street trading profession sold different goods like posters, betel buts, biri, cigarettes, newspapers, steel wools, socks, audio cassettes, ice-cream, clips, coconuts, fruits and such other items of chemicals at door to door and at the street sides.

Causes of Accepting Employment from Childhood

To know the reasons responsible for such an employment from childhood, table below reveals the opinion of these respondents regarding employment.

Table 13.10: Distribution of Respondents According to Cause of Employment

Sl. No.	*Cause*	*Total*	*Percentage*
1	Poverty	36	36.00
2	To assist parents	48	48.00
3	To earn their own living	8	8.00
4	Better than doing nothing	2	2.00
5	Other reasons	6	6.00
	Total	**100**	**100.00**

Table 13.10 shows that 36 per cent directly mentioned poverty as the main cause of their employment and thus compelled them to go for work. Forty-eight per cent reported because of the socio-economic compulsions they assist parents to work to support the needs of the family. Eight per cent mentioned that they accepted work to earn their own living. Two per cent stated that instead of moving on to streets it was better to earn than doing nothing. While 6 per cent admit for various reasons like family burden on them and others says to work for own fooding and clothing.

Among the respondents who stated poverty as the main reason of accepting employment from childhood the following tables reveal the fact mentioned by them.

Out of 36 per cent who mentioned poverty as the main cause, 20 per cent say that large family is the reason and makes them difficult to get sufficient food. Six per cent reported that their father died who was the main earning hand in the family. Two per cent say it is because of the death of their mother and another 4 per cent because of the death of their parents who support them. While 4 per cent admitted that there is no male member in the family and thus compelled them to get employment.

Table 13.11: Distribution of Respondents According to Cause of Poverty

Sl. No.	*Cause*	*Total*	*Percentage*
1	Large family	20	20.00
2	Father died	6	6.00
3	Mother died	2	2.00
4	Parents' death	4	4.00
5	No other working male member in the family	4	4.00
	Total	**36**	**36.00**

Table 13.12 below gives us the idea on income of child labour in various occupations:

Table 13.12: Monthly Income of the Child Respondents

Sl. No.	*Income per month*	*Total*	*Percentage*
1	Without Payment	12	12.00
2	Up to Rs.50	22	22.00
3	Up to Rs.70	2	2.00
4	Up to Rs.100	12	12.00
5	Rs.100 to Rs.150	4	4.00
6	Rs.150 to Rs.200	18	18.00
7	Rs.200 to Rs.250	0	0.00
8	Rs.250 to Rs.300	6	6.00
9	Rs.300 and above	24	24.00
	Total	**100**	**100.00**

Table 13.12 shows that 12 per cent of the respondents are working without payment as they assist their family members in petty business. The major group of child labour 22 per cent earn below Rs. 50 per month selling *kwai* (betel nuts), cigarettes, audio cassettes and newspapers which is very low. Due to low remuneration these child labourers change their job very often. Most of these child labourers said that nobody forced them to

work but they willingly joined their particular line of profession. Two per cent earned below Rs. 70, 12 per cent earn below Rs. 100. Further, 4 per cent earn between Rs. 100 to Rs. 150, another 18 per cent earn between Rs. 150 to Rs. 200. The data collected shows that no child respondent found earning between Rs. 200. to Rs. 250 per month. Six per cent earn between Rs. 250 to Rs. 300. A large percentage of 48 per cent found earning between Rs. 300 and above per month.

Household Monthly Income

In many cases each household of the child respondents there are more than one earning member. As the family size grows the earners also increase. Hence, the study of monthly household income will give a clear picture of their economic conditions.

Table 13.13: Monthly Income of Household

Sl. No.	*Income in Rs.*	*Total*	*Percentage*
1	Below 500	0	0.00
2	500 to 600	4	4.00
3	600 to 700	6	6.00
4	700 to 800	10	10.00
5	800 to 900	18	18.00
6	900 and above	50	18.00
7	Don't know	10	10.00
8	Living alone	2	2.00
	Total	**100**	**100.00**

Table above shows that none is found earning below Rs. 500 per month. Of the total respondents 4 per cent earn Rs. 500 to Rs. 600, 6 per cent earn Rs. 600 to Rs. 700, 10 per cent earn Rs. 700 to Rs. 800, 18 per cent earn Rs. 800 to Rs. 900 per month. A large percentage 50 per cent earn more than Rs. 900 per month. While 10 per cent of the respondents mentioned they do not know the monthly income of the family and 2 per cent of the respondents live alone.

The low income is because of lack of regular work of family members and in many cases under-employment. Their family income is quite insufficient which compels the children to go to work to supplement their family income or to assist parents.

Indebtedness

Out of the total sample respondents only 6 per cent are indebted. This is evident that child labour in Shillong city are not forced to get employment. Most of the child labour who do employment is either they assist their parents or because of the earners of the family died or because they feel lazy to go to school or succumbing to their families financial constraints, they dropped out of school to earn a little more for their economically deprived families. Table below shows the indebtedness of the child labour.

Table 13.14: Indebtedness Among Child Labour

Sl. No.	*Amount*	*Total*	*Percentage*
1	Below 50	2	2.00
2	50 to 100	4	4.00
3	100 to 150	0	0.00
4	150 to 200	0	0.00
5	No debt	94	94.00
	Total	**100**	**100.00**

Table 13.14 reveals that only 2 per cent is having the debt below Rs.50 and another 4 per cent is having the debt between Rs.50 to Rs. 100. These children are to adjust within their limited income. Table 13.15 shows the distribution of indebted respondents according to their sources of borrowing.

It is found that 66.67 per cent of the respondents have borrowed money from their employers which is the easiest available source and to repay back the money, 33.33 per cent have borrowed money from their friends and relatives. None is found borrowed money from money lenders. Indebtedness is due to different causes as per the Table 13.16.

Table 13.15: Sources of Borrowing

Sl. No.	*Sources*	*Total*	*Percentage*
1	Friends and Relations	2	33.33
2	Employers	4	66.67
3	Money Lenders	0	0
	Total	**100**	**100.00**

Table 13.16: Causes of Debt

Sl. No.	*Cause*	*Total*	*Percentage*
1	To meet own expenses	2	66.66
2	For family needs	2	66.66
3	For medical expenses	2	66.66
	Total	**6**	**98.98**

The above table reveals that out of the total respondents who have borrowed money, 66.66 per cent each mentioned they have borrowed money to meet their own expenses like new dress, etc., another 66.66 borrowed money to meet the needs of the family and again 66.66 say they borrowed money for medical expenses for self and their family members.

Savings

Out of the total sample respondents 50 per cent who are conscious enough save something from their little income. Table below shows the savings of the child respondents.

Table 13.17: Savings of Child Respondents

Sl. No.	*Amount per month*	*At Home*	*Post Office*	*Bank*	*With Employer*
1	Up to Rs.5	28	—	—	—
2	Rs.5 to Rs.25	14	—	—	—
3	Rs.25 to Rs.50	—	—	—	—
4	Rs.50 to Rs.100	—	2	2	2
5	Rs.100 and above	2	—	—	—
Total		**44**	**2**	**2**	**2**
Percentage		**88**	**4**	**4**	**4**

Out of 50 per cent of the child respondents who can save money, 28 per cent can save only up to Rs. 5 per month; another 28 per cent save between Rs. 5 to Rs. 25 per month; another 6 per cent can save Rs. 50 to Rs. 100 and 2 per cent can save more than Rs. 100 per month.

Those who can save, 88 per cent of the respondents save their money at home; another 4 per cent save their money in the Post-Office; again 4 per cent save their money in the Bank and another 4 per cent save their money with their employers.

Hours of Work

Table 13.18 indicates the present conditions of child labour in Shillong city.

Table 13.18: Distribution of Working Children According to Working Hours per day Debt

Sl. No.	*Hours per day*	*Total*	*Percentage*
1	Below eight hours	26	26.00
2	Eight hours	18	18.00
3	Nine hours	8	8.00
4	Ten hours	12	12.00
5	Eleven hours	16	16.00
6	Twelve hours and above	20	20.00
	Total	**100**	**100.00**

Twenty-six per cent of child respondents are working below eight hours. Eighteen per cent are working for 8 hours per day. Eight per cent are working for nine hours per day and 12 per cent for ten hours per day. The data further reveals that 16 per cent of children are working for eleven hours and 20 per cent work for more than twelve hours per day.

Further, the data collected reveals that children engaged in household works are working for eleven to twelve hours per day and the children in hotels and restaurants have also worked for 9 to 12 hours. Boys engaged in garage and motor servicing, welding works, etc. are working for 9 to 11 hours.

Working Timing

The following table indicates the time at which these children start their work.

Table 13.19: Time at Which Children Start this Work

Sl. No.	*Timing*	*Total*	*Percentage*
1	5.00 a.m. to 6.00 a.m.	12	12.00
2	6.00 a.m. to 7.00 a.m.	6	6.00
3	7.00 a.m. to 8.00 a.m.	32	32.00
4	8.00 a.m. and after	50	50.00
	Total	**100**	**100.00**

Data collected reveals that 12 per cent of the child labour starts their work at 5.00 a.m. to 6.00 a.m. and finish their work by 6.00 p.m. Six per cent start at 6.00 a.m. to 7.00 a.m. and finish by 7.00 p.m. Another 32 per cent starts working at 7.00 a.m. to 8.00 a.m. and finish at 9.00 p.m. A large majority of 50 per cent starts their work at 8.00 a.m. and finish at 10.00 p.m. everyday. Out of which, 4 per cent finish their work at 11.00 p.m. and another 6 per cent mentioned that they finish their work at 12.00 p.m. or after 12.00 p.m. everyday.

The following table illustrates how many child respondents are enjoying holidays.

Table 13.20: Weekly Holidays

Sl. No.	*Respondents*	*Total*	*Percentage*
1	Those who enjoy weekly holidays	34	34.00
2	Who do not enjoy weekly holidays	52	52.00
3	Enjoy Sunday only	14	14.00
	Total	**100**	**100.00**

Only 34 per cent children who are employed enjoy weekly holidays. Fifty-two per cent mentioned of not getting this facility. Those children engaged in hotels and restaurants do not get weekly holidays. Children working in household work are not getting any holidays. While 14 per cent stated that they enjoy Sundays only.

Children employed at their own will or by their parents, whether they like their job or not is indicated here.

Table 13.21: Perception of the Job

Sl. No.	*Items*	*Total*	*Percentage*
1	Liking	64	64.00
2	Disliking	16	16.00
3	Neutral	20	20.00
	Total	**100**	**100.00**

Sixty-four per cent of the respondents like their jobs but 16 per cent do not like their jobs. Those who like their jobs are mostly employed in household works, restaurants, self-employments like collecting broken tins, iron, polythenes, etc. and street trading like selling posters, steel wool, *biri*, cigarettes and *kwai* (betel nut) and *chana*, and newspaper, hawkers, garage, mason work and assist their mothers in petty small shops. Those who do not like their jobs are also found engaged in restaurant, self-employment and street trading because of the monotonous nature of their jobs and they see for future prospects in them. The other 20 per cent of the respondents who are neutral to their jobs are mostly engaged in restaurants, motor servicing work, welding works, mason work and self-employment.

Table 13.22: Employers Attitude

Sl. No.	*Opinion*	*Total*	*Percentage*
1	Sympathetic	16	29.62
2	Hostile	8	14.82
3	Neutral	30	55.56
	Total	**4**	**100.00**

Here self-employed children in different occupations and street trading which accounts for 46 per cent of the respondents are not included. From others 29.62 per cent reported their employers are sympathetic to them but 14.82 per cent do not hesitate to tell against them as these employers are hostile to them for small mistakes. 55.56 per cent expressed the neutral attitude of their employers.

Future Expectations of Child Respondents

During investigation respondents were asked about their future plan and their expectations.

Table 13.23: Future Plan of Child Respondents

Sl. No.	*Plan*	*Total*	*Percentage*
1	To remain in the same job	10	10.00
2	To accept other job	44	44.00
3	To have own business	24	24.00
4	Wants to go back to school	4	4.00
5	Cannot decide	18	18.00
	Total	**100**	**100.00**

Above table reveals that 10 per cent of the respondents prefer to remain in the same job. This consists mainly children employed in household work and self-employment. Forty-four per cent expressed their desires to accept other jobs because of the hardships of the job and there are no future prospects in them. This includes mostly children in street trading, mason works and self-employed, etc. while 24 per cent of child labour decided to have their own business in future covers mainly boys employed in garage and motor servicing works, helping their mothers in petty business and restaurants. Another 4 per cent wish to go back to school if opportunity is given to them covers girls engage in household works. Whereas, 18 per cent of these respondents cannot decide their future plan of action consists of those engaged in restaurants, street trading, mason work and household work because of their small outlook.

Legal Awareness

Due to ignorance and illiteracy these children do not know about their rights. Table 13.24 shows the awareness of these children about their rights.

Table 13.24: Legal Awareness

Sl. No.	*Awareness*	*Total*	*Percentage*
1	Aware	16	16.00
2	Not aware	84	84.00
	Total	**100**	**100.00**

Table reveals that 84 per cent of the child respondents are not aware the existence of any legislative measures for regulating their employment and various measures for their welfare. Only 16 per cent stated that they have heard about the rights of the child but do not know what are the provisions for their benefit.

Major Findings

(1) The age-sex-wise distribution of the child respondents reveals that 70 per cent have entered into work at the age of nine. Forty-six per cent belong to the age-group of 8-12 years and 48 per cent have entered the present job at the age of 12-14 years and most of them are male children. About 6 per cent of them have entered the job at the age below eight years.

(2) Thirty-six per cent of the total 100 working children are illiterate and 26 per cent of them are semi-literate in the sense that they have education up to class three. Thus, the majority is illiterate. About 12 per cent of them were school drop-outs and only 26 per cent were attending schools while on the job.

(3) Eighty-four per cent of the child labourers are migrated from the rural areas from outside the district. Ten per cent have migrated from their native place to semi-urban areas of Shillong city; while 6 per cent are migrated to urban areas within the district to get employment.

(4) Sixty-two per cent of the child labourers doing labour work are from the families having more than 8 members in the family. Seventy-four per cent of the

child labour never attended the school or drop-outs because of poverty.

(5) Most of them, 90 per cent of these child labourers live with their parents in the scattered locality of Shillong city. Only a few live with their relatives.

(6) The income level-wise distribution of the working children shows that only 24 per cent get monthly income ranging from Rs. 300. A large majority of these child labourers get monthly income ranging from Rs. 50 to Rs. 100 and Rs. 100 to Rs. 200. Only 6 per cent of the working children are having the debt between Rs.50 to Rs. 100 which shows that child labourers in Shillong city are not forced to get employment.

(7) About 74 per cent of the child respondents have to work more than eight hours a day to earn such incomes. While 36 per cent of them work for 11 to 12 hours per day to earn their wages.

(8) Two things show in the relationship between working hours and income of the working children. First, in most cases a large number of children work for longer hours per day and secondly, a large number of them get less income by putting in the same working hours per day. Table 13.12 and Table 13.18 show the extent of under payment of child labour.

(9) Only 34 per cent of the child respondents who are employed enjoy weekly holidays and 52 per cent do not get this facility while 14 per cent enjoy Sundays only.

(10) Sixty-four per cent of these working children like their jobs but the rest do not like their jobs and some are neutral. Those who like the jobs are mostly children engaged in self-employment, street trading and helping their mothers in petty business.

(11) The perception and attitude of the working children about their job reveals that they do not have preference or choice, except to work for wages on account of poverty and socio-economic compulsions prevailing among them and their families.

(12) Lack of a stable family life, single-parent, up bringing, smoking and drinking of a father affects the child.

(13) No legislative measures have reached these children to save them from exploitation. As majority of them, 84 per cent do not know about the legislative measures for regulating their working conditions and providing them welfare services.

Conclusion and Suggestions

Briefly speaking, family problems, financial constraints and disinterest in studies have been attributed to discontinuing studies. According to the information compiled by the Labour Ministry, the incidence of child labour is closely related to the rate of school drop-outs. The report further mentioned that a large number of these drop-out children find wage employment of some kind.

In most cases, the low educational level of the children's parents may also influence the children to drop out. More than 80 per cent of the child workers are in the rural areas working on farms, etc. To keep the poor families survived they feel that having more children means more labourers. Many studies have over-emphasized the element of poverty. But field experience had shown that parents were eager to send their wards to school but in the absence of proper educational facilities, felt their children could better utilize their time in wage employment. Indifference at the educational level was thus a major reason for children dropping out of school and seeks employment.

To build a strong educational regime, it is essential to check the growth of child labour. Of late, various NGOs in the state have joined hands in a move to sensitise the state government about the increasing presence of child labour in the state. Therefore, the need of the hour is to build a 'mind set' that child labour should be eradicated within a specific time frame. This problem could be solved through interaction and co-operation between the government and non-government organisation, the child workers and the employers. Any strategy for the benefit of the child workers must have a focus and situational area specific guidelines emerging out of a consensus among all the major actors to address the nature of the problem.

The following are the suggestions for child labourers:

(1) There is a need to train the untrained primary school teachers through proper orientation and refresher course to retain school students and reduce drop-out rate.
(2) Another strategy is to ensure that all working children in the age-group 5-14 years of age are directly put into school under the Sarva Shiksha Abhiyan.
(3) It is for the society at large and the community at the local level to ensure that children are sent to school and not to the labour market.
(4) Efforts should be made to generate more jobs and raise the literacy level of the poor families so that on one hand, it obviates the need to send children to the labour market and, on the other, to sensitise the family to send them to school.
(5) The Government should develop and implement suitable rehabilitation strategies.
(6) The appropriate agencies should provide counselling to the parents and children.
(7) The school drop-outs may be identified and brought them back to school.
(8) The universities may develop appropriate life skills education programme and impart to these children.
(9) Provide short term continuing education programmes.
(10) Awareness programmes need to be given at the grass-roots level.
(11) Advocacy programmes need to be given to the village headmen, opinion leaders, church elders, government officials, school teachers, NGOs, functionaries, etc.
(12) Your patient hearing.

To tackle the problem of child labour in the north-eastern region, the centre has introduced new measures under the scheme of National Child Labour project. The aim of this project is to ensure that the school drop-out rate is brought to the minimum. This project aims to give special emphasis on those who are engaged in hazardous works. Except Meghalaya, four north-eastern states, Assam, Mizoram, Nagaland and Tripura would be covered under the new NCLP project.[7]

NOTES

1. *Shillong Times*, dated 19th February, 2004, p. 4.
2. *Ibid.*, dated 10th October, 2002, p. 4.
3. *Ibid.*, dated 19th February, 2004, p. 4.
4. *Ibid.*
5. *Ibid.*
6. *Meghalaya Guardian*, dated 20th September, 1994, p. 3.
7. *Shillong Times*, dated 17th January, 2006.

14

Solid Waste Management: Peoples Participation in Disposal of Shillong City Garbage

Shillong, the capital of Meghalaya is a hilly state in the North-Eastern part of India. The city is located at an altitude of 1945 metres (above MSL) and a number of rivers and streams that flow through the city. Shillong got its name from the Shillong Peak, which is considered as sacred and perhaps named after its discoverer as Shillong. Shillong, began to grow in 1864. Later on it became the capital of Assam till the emergence of Meghalaya. The state, has at present seven administrative districts and Shillong is the headquarters of East Khasi Hills district.

Very often Meghalaya referred to as the 'Scotland of the East' or Queen of Hill Stations due to its striking affinity with the mountain scenery of the Scottish highland. The Britishers christened it as "Mini London". Shillong is indeed, one of the most beautiful hill stations in the whole country. Many native rulers were fascinated to use the city as their summer resort.

Shillong urban area is criss-crossed by a number of mountains, streams and dotted with falls. The river with their tributaries, big and small, form an evenly distributed network of water ways in the city and its suburbs. Many of these streams flow throughout the year. These streams having sparkling water add to the beauty and charm of this enchanting hill station.[1] Many picnic spots were located by the side of these streams. Shillong, has had an average annual rainfall of 2.150 mm. Mawsynram, in the East Khasi Hills District, is the "wettest place" in the world.

As of now, these watercourses have been reduced to stinking sewers. Huge garbage of dumps on the streambeds acts like dams during the dry season. After rainstorm these streams look like conveyor belts for rubbish of the worst kind.[2]

One of the consequences of environmental awareness is the sea change in attitude towards waste management. Untreated waste is dumped at localities not far from urban areas. Thus, waste disposal has become increasingly difficult because land available for the dump is continuously encroached by urban sprawl.

After all what is waste? In simple language it is the useless, unwanted, unused or discarded materials comprising solid, liquid and gas components.

Experts opined that the main sources of solid waste management in Shillong can broadly be divided into domestic, commercial, institution and natural.[3] Domestic solid waste includes kitchen waste, paper cartons, rags, plastics, tin can, rubber, bones, leather, glass and other hazardous waste. Commercial wastes emanates from a variety of sources and include stores, tea stalls, business premises, godowns, meat or butcher shops, restaurants, barber shops, markets, hostels, slaughter houses, etc. and similar industrial units. Iewduh, Police Bazar, Polo Bazar, Keating Road are some of the important sources of such waste in Shillong. Waste generated from hospitals, clinics and nursing homes, school and colleges, banks, offices, public and community toilets are clubbed under the head of institutional wastes. Waste from hospitals referred to as "clinical waste" poses serious health harzards and danger to the environment. Natural waste includes waste from trees, plants, stray animals, dry leaves, flowers and carcasses of animals, etc.

Solid Waste Disposal: Case Study of Shillong

Shillong once known for its scenic beauty is now undergoing a drastic change due to its haphazard and unplanned growth. For over the years, lack of proper planning, unchecked haphazard growth and a tremendous increase in population has ensured that Shillong joined the ranks of the dirty and polluted cities in the country. Most of the pollution is caused by the vehicular emissions. Urbanisation, also has brought about evils like slums, thus contribute to growing pollution in the city. In Shillong, scientist recorded[4] that the stone quarrying, tree felling, indiscriminate growth of hotels, restaurants and vehicles, workshops and improper solid wastes are the main causes for environmental pollution in Shillong. The most unpleasant scene today is that, urban waste scattered all over. Metallic waste, plastic, rubber, old tyres, wastes from tyre retreading shops, human hair from the saloons, waste engine oil from the automobiles and soil dug out from the construction sites are just thrown into the valley and streams. Further, dumping of wastes around houses, restaurants, tea and snacks stalls besides food joints have resulted in the increasing health and environmental problems in the town. Practice of rampant dumping of refuse on the streets after putting them into the polythene bags with solid refuse into the public drains often lead to clogging of the drains. Shillong produces hundred tonnes of waste everyday. The waste is often carelessly dumped in heaps in the city, thereby, giving the city a dismal look. Significantly, it is this waste which poses serious health hazard.

Simultaneously, it is distressing to note that the mechanism of waste collection and disposal is totally inadequate in Shillong. Wastes lying on roadsides, street bins piles up open spaces are a common feature. Wastes collected from various localities in Shillong are quite often disposed of into rivers or even in drains without any consideration to the adverse effect it might have on the environment.

Another factor to be mentioned here is the disposal of plastic wastes in Shillong. Rampant usage of polythene bags had led to the choking of drains and *nallahs* thereby, created health hazards since plastics are non-bio-degradable. Indiscriminate use of plastics resulted in the huge quantities of plastic waste in the environment. This, in turn poses serious environmental problems. It is to be noted that Shillong falls under a special category among the various cities and towns of the country where there is hardly any organised waste disposal system. The number of rag pickers is almost negligible to handle the condition of solid waste generated in the city.

There is no industrial unit to recycle the plastics if collected by the rag pickers and other wastes disposers.

As per the NEERI, Nagpur Report on the 'Planning of Solid Wastes Management at Shillong', 1991, about 38,528 tonnes of garbage is generated in Shillong from the municipal and cantonment area per day. Plastics range only from 0.47 to 1.47 per cent. Thus, about 171.08 to 669.39 kgs of plastics is generated in the city per day.[5] In Shillong, no ready made solution is available for disposal of plastics. In view of this, in April 1998, the state government requested the MPCB to submit a report on the disposal of plastic wastes and the possible ways to dispose them. The Board in its report suggested banning the use of polythene bags for the preservation of the environment.[6]

Organisation, Management and Disposal of Solid Waste

The greater Shillong area consists of Shillong Municipal Board, Cantonment Board and on area under the control of the *Syiem* of Mylliem for which necessary organisation exists. It also includes four townships which have no proper solid waste management system.

Shillong Municipal Board has been in existence for more than 97 years. The area under Municipal Board covers 10.36 sq.kms. and had a population of 1,32,876 as per 2001 census. The Health Officer is the head of the solid waste activities and is assisted by senior Sanitary Inspector and Sanitary Inspectors. The area of the Municipal Board is divided into twenty-seven wards and group them into five zones. A solid waste management in Bara Bazar area is under the control of *Syiem* of Mylliem. The conservancy staff manages the collection of refuse in the market area and manages to transport by using one truck. Besides Municipal Board Cantonment Board and four townships are also included in the development authority.

Collection of Solid Waste

In Shillong, the garbage is collected by adopting the community bin system. Altogether, 105 community dustbins and stone slab dustbins with 32 open spots were scattered over the twenty seven wards. Collection is normally done every morning between 8.00 a.m. to 11.00 a.m. and between 2.00 p.m. to 4.00 p.m. in the afternoon, but this is normally not done. Street cleaning is carried out by sweepers for specific areas of different localities. The sweepers are expected to collect the sweeping and dump it at the nearest community dustbins. But this is not done so. Due to the hilly terrain, the collection of refuse poses problems and hence conical cane baskets, spade, etc. are used.

Earlier Municipal Board also collect night soil from dry latrines located within municipal area. The night soil is transported in trolley-mounted tanker to Mawïong dumping ground and dumped in trenches for conversion of night soils into manure. At present, this is non-functional.

Transportation

The refuse collected at specific points is removed by the open body trucks and tractor-trailers. In each truck five labourers are provided who travel and help unload it at the disposal side. At present, there are eleven garbage cleaner trucks and four tractors deployed for carrying solid waste.[7] These vehicles carry approximately 30 tonnes of solid waste from municipal area to the dumping yard.

Disposal

The wastes from the municipal area is disposed of at a 18 acre trenching ground located 7 kms. away from the city on the Shillong-Guwahati road. Composting with night soil has been practiced since 1974. The produced compost is sold at a rate of Rs. 40-60 per metric tonne. As the disposal is carried out with no proper specific guidelines, flying breeding, smell and odour problem are noticed.

Problems Encountered

Although the Municipality is responsible for the "solid waste" collection and disposal, it lacks inadequate facilities, infrastructure and resources to provide service in area other than the care area. In Shillong experts opined[8] that there are potential health hazards and risks associated with the poor management of solid waste. They, however, pointed out that people living near the dumping sites are susceptible to respiratory problems, diarrhoea, skin, eye infection and other diseases. Sweepers and waste pickers are also prone to such diseases since they do their work without any masks and gloves. The burning of waste also contributes to air pollution and respiratory infections. Another problem, arising due to the dumping of waste is the pollution of drinking water. The pollution can cause diarrhoea, gastroenteritis, cholera, typhoid, dysentery and jaundice. As per the survey conducted by NEERI, Nagpur, 1991, the population of greater Shillong area will be 5,20,548 by 2011 A.D. and it is estimated to generate 197.3 tonnes of wastes per day.[9]

Failure of Municipal Board in Disposal of City Garbage

The present system of solid waste management in Shillong has not been properly designed and operated. As per the NEERI Report, Municipal Board vehicles perform two trips per day and *Ïewduh* vehicles three trips per day. But in practice only a small number of vehicles made two trips per day and the remaining vehicles made only one trip. Thus, the average refuse removal from municipal area was 34.718 tonnes per day only.[10] Usually, municipal truck move around the localities in Shillong to remove the solid wastes only two days in a week, i.e., Monday and Saturday. But the timing is not regular. Recently, two municipal trucks are plying on Sunday only in selected localities for removal of wastes. On the other hand, the provision of brooms, *thapa* and frequency of its replacement in the present system are adequate. Further, the existing system of the Municipal Board is not able to keep the city clean mainly due to inadequacy of staff.[11]

Role of Non-government Agencies Relating to Issues Concerning Environment and Health

NGOs can play a very important role in the disposal of city garbage. They can make the people aware of the problems created by unplanned management of city garbage. They can educate the people regarding the issues concerning environment and enlisting their active participation and co-operation.

In Shillong, various NGOs, institutions, social and cultural organisations observed the World Environment day every year since 1998 by organising meetings and seminars to focus on environment issue. In 1998, for the first time in Shillong, a cleaning drive was launched in all the schools and colleges from 1st to 5th June in different localities of Shillong. All educational institutions were informed to collect waste paper and plastic for recycling. Arrangement was made for a municipal truck to move around the localities of Shillong between 11.00 a.m. to 3.00 p.m. to collect waste gathered as part of collaboration with the Urban Affairs Department and Environment Task Force.[12] Meantime, the Meghalaya Environment Active Legislators (MEAL), Shillong, launched an awareness campaign among the people on the need for keeping the waters clean.[13] A massive cleaning drive by the MEAL to clean the streams and rivers was held on June 27, 1998 as the first phase of the drive. In this drive, youth organisation extended their helping hand for cleaning. All traders within the stream course employ two volunteers for the cleaning drive in order to restore again the "lost glory of Shillong—Scotland of the East".[14] During the second phase operation conducted in July 1998, the MEAL visited some of the dumping sites and appealed to the resident including village headman, local youth organisation, students' union of the areas concerned to join hands together in making the drive a success. The MEAL, however, directed all wine stores in Shillong to sell liquor only to those people in empty bottles littered in order to help curb pollution. At the same time, the

MEAL appeal to the public to refuse plastic bags but instead ask for paper bags to be supplemented by the MEAL. This in turn will help to generate employment to a large section of the local educated unemployed youth of the State.[15] In a survey conducted by the Khasi Students' Union (KSU), Shillong on the elements contributing to the destruction of the environment, the survey found that polythene was one such element as it is non-biodegradable. The KSU, in a letter submitted to the State Government, urged to ban the use of polythenes in the State and paper can be used as a substitute.[16]

Subsequently, to save the environment and control pollution, the Laban *Durbar*, one of the local *Durbar* in Shillong in its meeting held on June 3, 1998, outlined the dangers of pollution and wanton destruction of forest wealth. To this effect, a resolution was adopted to clean the Umkynrud river, road side shops, its surroundings and also the dustbins, etc.[17]

Another newly formed organisation known as "Shillong We Care" also launched a cleaning drive in some localities in Shillong for building up a clean and healthier environment in the Shillong streets.[18] After the promulgation of the Environment Protection Act, 1986, the Ministry of Environment and Forests, Government of India, issued a notification making it mandatory to hold environmental public hearings for developmental projects. The aim is to bring about the involvement of the people at the grassroots level. In view of this, it may be pointed out here, that the CEE, North-East in collaboration with "Shillong We Care", organised a public hearing on Environment and Development on 5 July, 1996. The hearing highlighted various issues of becoming an environmental disaster by creating awareness on those issues to grassroots groups, regional bodies and concerned citizens.[19]

People's Participation in Disposal of City Garbage

People's participation is necessary for the effective solid waste management of the cities. The Shillong Municipal Board has been making efforts from time to time to improve collection of garbage through increased frequency and deploying more vehicles. The Board, on its own, may find difficulty in refraining people from throwing garbage on the road. They, however, felt that taking up such programmes at city level may not be possible and the Board, on its own, cannot make much headway unless participation of the community is ensured. In May 1994, the Shillong Municipality and the Urban Affairs Department along with the Meghalaya Environmental and Wild Life Society conducted a survey in Lummawrie, one of the localities in Shillong, for community solid waste management. There were 264 households in Lummawrie and only few households were not accessible by road. A survey was carried out by the local volunteers who visited door to door. To know how garbage is being collected. During the visit, the volunteers distributed pamphlets urging the residents to co-operate with the municipality in collection of garbage on lines suggested by them.[20] Those households which are not connected by road expressed certain difficulties. These households volunteered to carry the waste in the plastic bags or in the containers to the nearest collecting point. According to arrangement made, the Municipal truck start collecting garbage from each household at 6.30 a.m. and the entire work is completed by 8.00 a.m. just before the schools open. Interestingly, with their active participation, the individual households keeping garbage in front of their houses early in the morning either in plastic bags or in containers. This collection of garbage by the community has brought about a sea change in the said locality. The local volunteers thus contributed to this success and ensured the locality to remain clean. At present, the households are keeping the garbage for two days inside their houses. On the appointed day they keep in front of the houses to be collected by the municipal staff.[21] With the success of the people's participation and the community involvement in Lummawrie, the system has been extended to nearly all the localities in Shillong. Thus, involvement of community is vital for success of any waste collection system.

With regard to the role of women organisation in the disposal of city garbage, Ka Lympung ki Seng Kynthei (KLKSK), a coordinating body of twenty-one women organisations from different localities of Shillong, organised a one-day awareness campaign on "Women's Role in Waste Utilization" on May 13, 1995 at Shillong. To this effect, an exhibition of items made out of waste materials was depicted to arouse the interest among the school children and the public in general. Altogether, eleven schools and fifteen women organisations of Shillong participated in the campaign. Two hundred forty-five and sixty-five items were prepared by schools and women organisations from waste products. Interestingly, people from all walks of life participated in the programme including the local headmen, MLAs, etc. This active participation and cooperation of various schools and organisations in Shillong made the campaign a very lively one. Meantime, two sessions of talk on "Women's role in environment amelioration", "Role of women in waste utilization and how to keep one's environment clean in the context of being socially useful" and the "Role of women and waste utilization in the context of being creative" were discussed.[22] The occasions, however, shows the sincere concern of the organisation on the degradation of the environment, deforestation and other environmental problems.

Future Proposal for Management of Garbage Disposal

There are various methods which can be best utilized for effective solid waste management in Shillong. These methods are already in operation in western and developed countries of the world. The various methods to be suggested here are: (i) Recycling of solid waste; (ii) Sanitary landfill; (iii) Segregation; and (iv) Composting of Bio-degradable wastes.

Recycling: Most household garbage is recycled. Paper, plastic, metal, glass and rags can be used in various manufacturing processes. In Shillong, there is hardly any organised waste disposal system. There is no industrial unit to recycle the plastic if collected by the rag pickers and other waste disposers.

Sanitary Landfill: The process basically consists of laying the waste material in a planned manner, then compacting the layer and finally, rule covering it with soil. In Shillong, the refuse and night soil is disposed of at the 7 acres trenching ground. Composting trenches are available and compost was produced. But sale of compost is much less. No proper sanitary land filling is carried out, though labourers are working at the landfill.

Segregation: Most household garbage contains many things that can be used. We often render them totally useless by dumping them along with other waste. We could make our beginning by segregation our garbage into useful and totally useless materials. There are other items in the garbage, which are generally classified as 'road waste'. To avoid this, we can segregate even road waste from our garbage, and hand it over to the rag picker. This enables them to earn their livelihood in a safer and healthier manner while contributing to save the environment by recycling.

Composting of Bio-Degradable Waste: This is one of the oldest methods of recycling. Organic wastes can be buried in the soil to make compost or humus, the rich black dirt formed by the decaying of animals and vegetable wastes. Compost helps the soil in retaining more plant nutrients over a longer period in controlling the weed growth. This is a common practice in Shillong.

Conclusion and Recommendations

The method of collection, transportation and disposal of garbage adopted by the civic authorities in the cities take specific guidelines, which is through dustbins, is not efficient. The number of dustbins is far from satisfactory. Generally, household wastes are disposed of within the compound of the individual houses. Even, if the householders throw the garbage in the dustbins, the garbage spills around the dustbins, thereby making the area filthy and unapproachable. It is also seen that the conservancy staff while taking out refuse from dustbins leave behind small pieces of waste materials which become a breeding ground for bacteria to grow and become potential health hazard. Further, no proper sanitary land filling is carried out at the landfill. In Shillong, the collection of waste is not from individual houses but from dustbins or open roadside points. Due to narrow streets provision of dustbins is a problem as it tends to disrupt the traffic.

On a careful analysis of the data and information collected, following suggestions may be made for collection, transportation and disposal of solid wastes in Shillong:

(1) House-to-house collection system should be introduced on a large scale.
(2) Narrow roads not approachable by municipal trucks, small cycles with trailer may be provided for collection of sewage from households.
(3) Areas which are accessible by footpaths, garbage may be collected by municipal staff from each house and payment will be made by the householder.
(4) Segregation of refuse into various constituents such as stone, paper, plastics, hay and straw, rags, etc. for recycle must be carried out at source.
(5) To ensure active participation and cooperation of all the citizens as well as the municipal workers local committees may be set up to educate the people about civic sense.
(6) Incentives for the cleanest ward must be provided.
(7) One truck should be provided to cater to the need of the each locality. Whenever the trucks are full, the cleansing staff should cover by a tarpaulin.
(8) Mass awareness programme through various NGOs' activities is essential for proper collection and disposal of waste management.

(9) Identify the key areas where attention must be given. Ways and means to recycle the waste materials must be attempted and to set up a plastic recycling unit.

(10) Social scientists have a great role to play in reorienting the social awareness programme.

NOTES

1. See "Basic Factors of Meghalaya", Directorate of Information and Public Relations, Meghalaya (n.d.).
2. See "Sprucing Up Shillong Streams", *Meghalaya Guardian*, Vol. III, No. 194, dt. July 19, 1992, p. 1, also see "Umkhrah-Yesterday, Today and Tomorrow", *Meghalaya Guardian*, Vol. IX, No. 89, dated April 1, 1994, p. 4.
3. See "Proper Waste Disposal Mechanism Still Left Wanting", *Meghalaya Guardian*, dated November 21 and December 1, 1997, p. 1.
4. *Meghalaya Guardian*, Vol. IX, No. 175, dated June 29, 1998, p. 1.
5. Final Report on "Planning for Solid Waste Management at Shillong", NEERI, Nagpur, 1991. Published by the Government of Meghalaya, Urban Affairs Department, Shillong, pp. 20-30.
6. See "Plastics: The City's Major Pollutions", *Apphira News*, Vol.IV, No. 357, dated June 29, 1998, p. 1.
7. Data is collected from the Shillong Municipal Board Office, Shillong.
8. *Meghalaya Guardian*, dated November 30, 1997, p.1.
9. Final Report on "Planning for Solid Waste Management at Shillong", NEERI, Nagpur, 1991, *op. cit.*, p. 30.
10. *Ibid.*, p. 23.
11. *Ibid.*, p. 31.
12. See "Cleaning Drive", *Meghalaya Guardian*, Vol. IX, No. 145, dated May 30, 1998, p. 1.
13. *Apphira News* (Daily News), Vol. IV, No. 308, dated May 10, 1998, p.1 .
14. See "Meal to Launch Cleaning Drive of Umshyrpi Stream", *Meghalaya Guardian*, Vol.IX, No. IX, No. 171, dated June 25, 1998, p. 1.
15. *Op. cit.*, No.187, dated July 11, 1998, p. 1.
16. See "KSU Urges Government to Ban Polythene", *Meghalaya Guardian*, Vol. IX, No. 148, dated June 2, 1998, p. 1.

SECTION V

Administration of Primary Education

15

Performance of Primary Education by the KHADC in Meghalaya

The educational structure of any country starts with primary education. A strong foundation for education is to be laid at this stage and the teachers at the primary level have a pivotal role to play. The objectives of achieving education for all, enrolment, retention and continuation of children are all depending upon the primary school teachers at the grassroots level. The present investigation is an effort to study the performance of primary education by the Khasi Hills Autonomous District Council (KHADC) in Meghalaya.

As per paragraph 6 of the Sixth Schedule to the Constitution of India, the District Council for an autonomous district, may establish, construct or manage primary schools and prescribe the language and the manner in which primary education is to be imparted in the primary schools under its control in the district.

Although the erstwhile United Khasi-Jaintia Hills District Council came into existence on 27th June, 1952, till 31st March, 1962, the Government of Assam at the request of the District Council had managed primary education in the district. On 1st April, 1962, the management of primary education was transferred from the State Government of Assam to the United Khasi-Jaintia Hills Autonomous District Council. At the time of transfer, there were altogether 66 permanent Government Lower Primary Schools with 99 teachers and 86 Junior Basic Schools with 159 teachers respectively with two Assistant Sub-Inspectors and their Peons at the time. In addition to these there were also other teachers under different scheme whose services were terminated by the government. The erstwhile government lower primary teachers enjoy the pay and all other allowances as admissible from time to time to government employee. But, the aided lower primary teachers enjoyed the pay and daily allowances only. As such, there were two categories of teachers, the temporary and the permanent teachers. The permanent teachers were sent to the council service as on deputation and all the services of all the temporary teachers were terminated before they were place at the disposal of the Council.[1]

Even before the transfer of primary education, the Council had established 99 regular schools and 17 Government Aided schools. The expenditure for these schools were met from the Council own resources. According to the Council there were 518 regular schools and 689 aided schools which were taken over from the Government of Assam. The total number of schools under the control of the Council in 1979 was 1,323 for both regular and aided schools and 2,150 teachers. From 1979, till 1984 only a few more schools came under the control of the Council. By 1987, there were 2,543 teachers and 32,000 students in the District Council primary schools.

When the Assam Government handed over primary education to the Council on 1st April 1962, it had shouldered the full financial commitments involved. That is the District Council was not called upon to shoulder financial responsibility from its own resources. Grants sanctioned by the government were sufficient to meet the maintenance cost of both the inspecting staff and the primary teachers under the control and management of the District Council.[2]

Every year since 1962, the District Council had to submit to the government an estimate of the grant necessary to meet the expenses of the management of primary schools and after scrutinising the estimate, the government released the grant in quarterly instalments. Thereafter, the District Council submits to the government a Utilisation Certificate on receipt of each instalment. The same principle was in the early years under the Meghalaya Government. Since the time of transfer of primary education till 1982-83 the management of primary education in the KHADC had been very smooth without any complaint from any quarter. But subsequently, there had been delay in releasing and short fall of maintenance grants. During the end of 1982, constraints in the KHADC began to register a short fall. To meet the deficit, the KHADC had to strain its own meagre resources. The manner of releasing grants by the Government in instalment basis does not provide the Council with the opportunity to make payment on a month-by-month system either to the inspecting staff or teachers. The administration of primary education by the KHADC became more complicated when grants for a further period were released while withholding grants for another period.[3]

It has been an admitted fact that the primary school teachers serving in schools controlled and managed by the KHADC had not been paid their salaries for several months and non-payment of their arrear pay arising out of the Revised Pay Rules, 1980. Hence a crisis in the administration of primary education by the Council had arisen. The failure of the KHADC to make payment of salary to the primary school teachers led the teachers to resort to demonstration and hunger-strike to demand prompt payment of their dues. According to the Meghalaya Government, the State Government had already sanctioned Rs.61,60,448.00 to the KHADC for meeting the arrear pay of the teachers due to revision of pay scale and matters connected with the running of primary schools. But the KHADC it was alleged, had diverted the money for other purposes thereby denying the poor teachers of their pay for several months.[4]

On 5 August, 1983 a meeting was held between the Minister of Education and the CEM of the Council, which was also attended by the officers of the Education Department of the Government and the Council respectively. At this meeting, it was decided that the scrutiny of the estimate for 1982-83 should be done jointly by the officers of both the Government and Council. On 16 August, 1983 the officers of both the Government and the Council met to assess the KHADC requirements for the year 1982-83. In the meeting there were charges and counter-charges between the State Government and the KHADC.[5]

Subsequently, a meeting between the CEM of the Council, Late Mr. B. Wanniang and the Chief Minister of Meghalaya, Late Capt. W.A. Sangma was held on 3 November, 1983 under the Chairmanship of Mr. Grosswell Mylliemngap, the Minister, Power and Transport, etc. At this meeting, it was made clear that further maintenance grants to KHADC for payment of salary of primary school teachers would be released only on opening of the Second Personal Ledger Account (PLA) for transaction of the aforesaid grants. At this meeting, the Minister for Power, Transport requested the CEM of the KHADC to agree to open the Second PLA to enable the smooth flow of funds from the State Government.[6]

There had been a long tussle between the State Government and the KHADC over the question of Second PLA[7] At one time even the Accountant General of Meghalaya had intimated the KHADC about the opening of Second PLA[8] The Meghalaya Government was also very firm on this condition which was a shock to the KHADC.[9] On 12th December, 1983, the CEM of the KHADC wrote to the Chief Minister of Meghalaya thus:

> "Further it will not be out of place to state that at the initial stage of the transfer of primary education to the control of the District Council during 1961-62 when the tribal areas department at that time was under your ministership, the question of opening the Second Personal Ledger Account in respect of Education Fund of this Council was raised by the government often having properly examined this matter intimated this Council, by the then Secretary-in-charge of the tribal areas department, Shri V.B. Vaghaiwalla, ICS that it was unnecessary for opening the Second PLA in view of paragraph 7 of the Sixth Schedule to the Constitution of India".[10]

The Executive Committee of the KHADC as a whole, had met and apprised the Chief Minister personally a number of times about the requirement of funds. But the Executive Committee of the KHADC were told that unless the Second PLA was opened no further grants would be released by the government. This was a blow to the Council.[11] The KHADC, rejected the government proposal for the opening of such an account and hence there was deadlock and complete disruption in the management of primary education.

This controversy over the payment of salary to the primary school teachers had culminated in the appointment by the Meghalaya Government of a one-man Commission of inquiry under paragraph 14 of the Sixth Schedule to the Constitution of India to inquire into the dislocation in the management of the primary education in the KHADC. The Government of Meghalaya by the Notification No. DCA/135/83/1 dated 20 December, 1983, appointed a one-man Commission of inquiry wherein the Notification states that "whereas the Governor of Meghalaya is satisfied that there is dislocation in the management of primary education in the Khasi Hills Autonomous District and it is expedient to appoint a Commission to enquire and report thereon".[12] Therefore, the Government of Meghalaya in exercise of the powers conferred by and under paragraph 14 of the Sixth Schedule to the Constitution of India appointed a Commission consisting of Shri S.K. Dutta, Ex-Chief Justice of the Gauhati High Court to enquire and report about the aforesaid dislocation and to suggest remedial action.

The Commission headed by S.K. Dutta invited views and suggestions. The Commission, however, received several memoranda from the District Council, All Meghalaya Primary School Teachers' Association, East and West Khasi Hills and the Lower Primary School Teachers' Association (APSTA). The Commission also received nearly one hundred letters from individual teachers ventilating their grievances mostly about non-payment of their salaries. Since the time at the disposal of the Commission was very short, the Commission headed by S.K. Dutta decided to rely on facts and figures collected by the experienced Five-Men Commission two each from the government as well as the Council respectively in addition to the Chairman.[13]

The Commission after examining all the memoranda submitted by the KHADC and the APSTA held the view in its report that there was no provision in the Sixth Schedule imposing any obligation on the State Government to make any financial grant to the Council for the management of primary education. Further, the Commission pointed out that clause (d) of sub-paragraph 3 of paragraph 8 of the Sixth Schedule authorised the Council to lay and collect taxes for the maintenance of schools. As such, the Commission held the view that no such tax had been levied and no attempt had been made by the council to find money from their own resources to meet the expenditure on primary education in excess of the total contributions from the State Government.[14]

On the other hand, the Commission found that the government paid only for the salaries of teachers and the inspecting staff and their peons. The Commission also stated that there was an allegation that the inspecting staff hardly inspected the schools. Their services were utilised by the council for office work. According to the Commission, if the allegation was true, the grants for maintaining the inspecting staff was frustrated. Thus, the Commission held the view that the money paid by the government for inspection work was diverted to get other kinds of work done. The Commission was also quite clear that the council did not supply the schools even cheap and essential articles like chalks, dusters, registers and blackboards etc. Thus, the Commission held the view that either the claim of the council was false or money provided for contingency had been misappropriated.[15]

Meantime, the Commission felt that the policy of the government to write directly to the Accountant General for his approval to open the Second PLA was not justified. The Commission pointed out that there was no obligation on the part of the government to bear any expenditure on primary schools managed by the District Council. The Commission held the view that the State Government had every right to lay down conditions for giving the grant-in-aid provided the conditions were not inconsistent with any constitutional provision. However, the Commission felt that the allegation of the

Executive Committee of the KHADC that the direction of the government to open the Second PLA without consulting the Council was the indirect attempt of the government to have an overall control over primary education had no force. Also the Commission pointed out that the decision to open such an account was not behind the back of the Executive Committee as was evident from the DO letter dated 3rd December, 1983 from the Chief Minister to the CEM of the Council.[16]

On the basis of the above findings, the Commission expressed the view that there was no justification for the reluctance of the council to open a Second PLA. Instead, the Commission felt that the council should have welcomed the opening so that money meant for primary education was often used for some other purposes might be set at rest. In spite of all these the Commission found the misuse and misapplication of money by the KHADC granted by the Meghalaya Government for primary education. The Commission further found that the KHADC "had been guilty of misusing and misapplying money" received from the Government of Meghalaya.[17] The Commission held the view that the untimely release of the government grants was due to the failure of the council to submit their budget estimate in time and for not submitting the utilisation certificates regularly for the grants sanctioned by the Government. The Commission also pointed out that the council did not realise that the estimates submitted by the council had to be thoroughly scruitinised.[18]

Over all the above facts pointed out, the Commission recommended that the only way out from the then crisis in the management and control of primary education was for the government to take over the functions of primary education under paragraph 16(2) of the Sixth Schedule to the Constitution of India. The Commission in its recommendation states clearly that the taking over of primary education by the State Government was for a temporary period only. The Commission submitted its report to the government in January 1984. Accepting the recommendation, the Governor being satisfied that the situation had arisen in which the administration of primary education could not be carried on by the Council assumed to himself the administration of primary education for a period of six months with effect from 29 February, 1984. Accordingly, the Governor appointed the Administrator of Primary Schools to discharge the powers and functions with respect to the administration of primary education.[19]

The tussle between the KHADC and the administrator on primary education led the Governor of Meghalaya to further extend the term of the administration of primary education under the management of the administrator. The extension of taking over by the Governor from time to time for a period of three months or six months led the teachers' association to demand the complete taking over of the management of primary schools by the State Government.[20] The extension of the management of primary education by the administrator from time to time had embarrassed the teachers' association. In a meeting held on 12 September, 1986 between the Chief Minister and the CEM of the Council it was decided to hand over the administration of primary schools to the Council. The meeting decided that the arrear pay of all the primary teachers be borne by the government pending final settlement of account between the District Council and the Government. Meanwhile, on 23rd September, 1986, the APSTA in a letter to the Minister of Education, Government of Meghalaya demanded that in the overall interest of primary education in Khasi Hills, primary education must be taken permanently by the Government of Meghalaya.[21]

In spite of the teachers' association demand, the Government of Meghalaya, suddenly on 25 September, 1986, had revoked with immediate effect the orders of taking over the administration of primary education in Khasi Hills. Immediately, the following day the KHADC assume to itself the administration of primary education from the State Government of Meghalaya. The Council also took over the powers and functions vested in the Council as per paragraph 6(1) of the Sixth Schedule. The CEM in a letter to the Chief Minister on 27 October, 1986, while appreciating the realisation of the State Government for solving the purpose for which primary education was taken over, stated since the outstanding dues of primary teachers had not fully been cleared by the government, the Council had rendered practically impossible to exercise the function as provided in paragraph 6(1) of the Sixth Schedule. The CEM pointed out that the handing and taking over of primary education should be in clean slate. Since the administrator could not hand over all the information required by the Council, therefore, the CEM of the Council in a letter to the Chief Minister on 29 October, 1986 requested the government to take further steps to consider the settlement of all outstanding dues which would be meted out accordingly.[22] Thus, the period from 26 September, 1986 to 28 October, 1986 was the period in which neither the State Government nor the KHADC had in actual control and management of primary schools. Hence, in contrary the Governor of Meghalaya being satisfied that the situation had arisen, assumed to himself the administration of primary education as per paragraph 16(2) of the Sixth Schedule with immediate effect from 29 October, 1986 to 29 April, 1987 for a further period of six months. Thus the teachers' demands were partly achieved. The Governor again extended the operation of the initial order for a further period of six months with effect from 29 April, 1987. Since no solution could come out to solve the problem on 29 October, 1987, the Governor of Meghalaya had further extended the administration of primary education for another six months with effect from 29 October, 1987 to 29 April, 1988.

Finally, on 22 April, 1988, the State Government requested the Council to let the government know whether the KHADC was ready to take back primary education. In giving a reply to the government, the Council stated that the matter would be taken up by the Council. Despite the desirability of returning the primary education to the Council, the State Government of Mehalaya, all of a sudden on 17 August, 1988 intimated the CEM that the State Government without revoking the notification of 28 April, 1988, informed the KHADC that the State Government had transferred the administration of primary education without any arrangement.[23] Contrary, the CEM of the Council stated that the handing over would be in accordance with paragraph 16(2) of the Sixth Schedule. The same way the State Government had taken over the schools from the District Councils. On questioning the procedure, the CEM pointed out that it was his duty to take over as per the constitutional provisions. He, however, insisted that the handing over procedure would have to meet the requirements of the provisions under the Sixth Schedule.[24]

Without the consideration of the suggestion of the CEM on 31 August, 1988, the KHADC was informed that the State Government had handed over the control and management of primary education to the Council with effect from 17 August, 1988. The letter directed that the salaries of the teachers be paid up to 17 August, 1988 without due observance of the formalities and procedures of handing over primary education.[25] On 9 September, 1988, the Deputy Chief Minister, Mr. D.D. Lapang invited the CEM of the Council that as spelt out in the White Paper on Education, 1988 the government had decided not to invoke paragraph 15(2) for temporary taking over of primary schools after expiry of the present term but to retain to the Council on condition that they should shoulder the entire financial liability from their own resources. He also stated that the new policy decision would naturally imply termination of earlier arrangement and practices.[26]

Meanwhile the CEM of the Council in a letter to the State Government on 15 September, 1988, requesting the government to hand over the management of primary education according to the decision arrived at on 12 September, 1988 that arrear pay of teachers be borne by the State Government. The Chief Minister, however, with reference to the said letter, pointed out to the CEM of the Council that since the KHADC had not accepted, the offer then stands withdrawn and the existing arrangement would continue.[27] The decision of the government was welcomed by the teachers' association in a letter to the Chief Minister of Meghalaya on 4th October, 1988. The government expressed the view that although the State Government asked the Council to take over the schools, there was no response from the Council.[28]

In view of the fact that the KHADC had refused to take over primary education without fulfilling certain conditions by the government, the government had to continue managing primary schools in the State. Since then the administration of primary education by the Council was under the control and management of the State Government of Meghalaya and it continues till today. Thus the affairs of the control of primary schools and primary education had become a controversial affair in the State of Meghalaya. However, the emphasis is not so much on the smooth conduct of the affairs of primary education, but on the salaries of the teachers. In this regard the school teachers prefer that the State Government should take over the management of primary schools permanently basically because of the financial viability.

NOTES

1. Memorandum dated 5th January 1984 from the Executive Committee, Khasi Hills District Council to Shri S.K. Dutta (Retired Chief Justice of Gauhati High Court), Chairman of the One-Man Commission to inquire into the dislocation in the primary education in the autonomous Khasi Hills District, p. 2.
2. Office of the Executive Committee, Khasi Hills Autonomous District Council, Shillong, *"The Khasi Hills Autonomous District Council in Retrospect"* dated 21 November 1987, p.10.
3. *Ibid.*, pp. 10-11.
4. See "Government to Deny District Council Shares", *Implanter*, Vol.XV, No.66, dated 20 August 1983, p. 1.
5. Dutta, S.K., *Report of the Commission of Inquiry on Primary Education in the Khasi Hills Autonomous District* (Shillong, Government Press, 1984), pp. 3-4.
6. *Ibid.*, p.10.
7. Letter to the Secretary, Government of Meghalaya, District Council Affairs Department, Shillong from H.W. Nongbet, Secretary, Executive Committee, KHADC, Shillong, No.DC.VI.Edn/Acctts/185/83/3, dated, Shillong, the 7 November, 1983.
8. Office of the Accountant General, Meghalaya etc. Shillong No.MTM/1-14/ML/82-83/10710, dated Shillong, November 1983.
9. Government of Meghalaya, Chief Minister of Meghalaya, letter No.DCA/75/83/PT.I/10 dated 3rd November 1983.
10. Office of the Executive Committee, Khasi Hills Autonomous District Council, Shillong, letter D.O. dated 12 December 1983.

11. Office of the Executive Committee, Khasi Hills Autonomous District Council, Shillong, *Report of the Executive Committee in the Matter of Primary Education*, p. 1.
12. Government of Meghalaya, DCA Dept. *Notification*, No.DCA.135/83/1 dated 20th December 1983.
13. Dutta, S.K., *Report of the Commission of Inquiry on Primary Education, op. cit.*, p. 2.
14. Dutta, S.K., *Report of the Commission of Inquiry on Primary Education in Khasi Hills, op. cit.* pp. 3-5.
15. *Ibid.*, pp. 5-6.
16. *Ibid.*, p. 7.
17. *Ibid.*
18. *Ibid.*
19. Orders of the Governor, *Notification* No.DCA.135/83/37 dated 29 February 1984, pp. 1-2.
20. See "Teachers, Demand to Takeover of L.P. Schools", *Implanter* (Shillong), Vol. XIX, dated 26 September 1984, p. 1.
21. See "All Primary School Teachers' Association, East & West Khasi Hills, H.Q. Shillong", dated 23 September 1986 in *News and Views* (an official organ of Meghalaya Bank Employees' Co-ordination Committee) Vol. 4, No. XV September 1986, p. 5.
22. Office of the Executive Committee, Khasi Hills Autonomous District Council, Shillong, *Letter of the CEM of the KHADC to the Chief Minister of Meghalaya*, dated 29 October 1986.
23. *Ka Jingpynshai Na Ka Executive Committee Khasi Hills Autonomous District Council: Halor Ka Jingpyniaid Ïa ka Skul Primary*, dated 27 August 1988, p. 3.
24. See "Hopingstone Lays Conditions for L.P. Schools Take Over", *Shillong Times*, Vol. XLIV, No. 5, dated 20 August 1988, p. 1.
25. *Report of the Chief Executive Member, Khasi Hills Autonomous District Council Regarding Primary Education*, pp. 1-2.
26. See "Management of Primary Education : Govt. Withdraws offer to Khasi Hills District Council", *Shillong Times*, Vol. XIV, No. 49, dated 5 October, 1983, p. 3.
27. *Ibid.*
28. *Shillong Times*, Vol. XLIV, No. 49, dated 5th October 1988, p.1.

Index